NOVA
THE COURAGE
TO
RISE

TRICIA JACOBSON
with Marie Beswick Arthur

Copyright @2021 Tricia Jacobson
All rights reserved in all countries and territories worldwide.
Published by Ingenium Books Publishing Inc.
Toronto, Ontario, Canada
Ingeniumbooks.com

Copyright fuels innovation and creativity, encourages diverse voices, promotes free speech, and helps create a vibrant culture. Thank you for purchasing an authorized edition of this book and for complying with copyright laws by not reproducing, scanning, or distributing this book or any part of it, in print or electronic form, without the express prior permission of the publisher. Please respect the hard work of the author and do not participate in or encourage the piracy of copyrighted intellectual property.
ISBNs
eBook: 978-1-989059-79-1
paperback: 978-1-989059-78-4
audiobook: 978-1-989059-80-7

Book cover design by Jessica Bell via Ingenium Books
Book formatting by Amie McCracken via Ingenium Books
Vector images: rawpixel, asmaarzq

Table of Contents

Letter to the Reader 1. 11
1. Aurora and Stella Count the Stars 15
2. Questlisting and Camping 21
3. Aurora and the Tree 33
4. Stella and the Spoon 59
5. Aurora and Stella Dig for Gold. 71
6. Pinky on Ditching Drama 91
7. Aurora the Advocate 99
8. Questlist Findings and the Strawberry Farm . . .119
9. Stories in the Stars 151
10. Aurora and her Birthmother 171
11. Stella Finds a Talisman 177
12. Stella Shares a Secret 193
13. The Courage to Rise 211
14. Aurora and Stella Make a Pact 237
Letter to the Reader 2. 241
Acknowledgments 245
About the Author. 247

To my husband, Greg, and daughters, Kailey, Reagan, Grace, and Allie—my loves.

Nova

An astronomical event causing the sudden appearance of a bright new star.

Aurora

A natural atmospheric light display in the sky seen in high-latitude regions close to the Arctic and Antarctic. The northern lights are called aurora borealis. The southern lights are aurora australis. Solar wind causes magnetic disturbances that result in brilliant, shifting, and colorful light shows.

Stella

The Latin word for star. Stella Polaris is the brightest star in the Ursa Minor constellation. Stella is also a crater on the moon.

LETTER TO THE READER 1

Imagine you are a river of love, flowing from mountain stream and glacial lake to the ocean, at your own pace, tumbling over rocks, and plunging over the edges of cliffs with confident energy and triumphant cheers in powerful freefall. The master of your journey, celebrating its clarity, delighting in the surprises.

The world needs more freefall learners. The world needs more you.

You are the author and artist of your life. I want you to make it your masterpiece.

Consider the story in this book as a mind makeover. No cosmetics required, this book and a reflective surface are the only supplies you need—don't worry about the reflective surface. When the time comes, you'll know where to look.

> **THERE IS A FREEDOM WITHIN YOU THAT WILL LEAD YOU TO GREATNESS.**

It is accessed by recognizing your individuality.

Greatness is not found in possessions, power, position, or prestige. Beauty is not found in following a brand whose message drains you. It is discovered in goodness, humility, service, and character. Goodness to yourself and then to others. A breath for yourself, then a breath for others.

Anyone can help others. Even those who need help can help others. Your contribution does not mean having to build an entire school, or feed an entire village, or start a foundation to lift a community out of poverty. This begins a ripple effect of goodness and generosity.

As you embrace and live the masterpiece of your life, may you:

- Flow with inspiration
- Embrace the miracle of life
- Be unapologetically you
- Light up every room
- Know when to rest
- Create with wild abandon
- Love and accept yourself
- Ask questions
- Recognize time wasters and social media energy drainers

- Never stop learning
- Celebrate laughter
- Give from the heart
- Learn from the faith of others
- Celebrate your own faith

Here's how it happened for Aurora and Stella.

Love, Tricia

1. AURORA AND STELLA COUNT THE STARS

How many stars you figure are up there, Aurora?

Too many to count, Stella. How's the sleeping bag?

More than a million? You should know. You're the smart one. I'm just the big mouth.

Okay, more than a million. Maybe a billion. And you're not that loud, Stella.

Who are we really?

Sometimes I wish I was one. A star. And everything was a restart.

Tricia Jacobson

Sometimes I wish I hadn't been born.

Don't say that, Stella. Hey, shall I be Mom?

I love it when you're Mom, Aurora. It's the best part of my day.

Okay, close your eyes. All the way, Stella. No cheating.

They are. They are closed.

Okay, I'm trusting you, Stella. Here we go. Once upon a time, high in a tree, in the middle of a little park in a big city, there was a bird sitting on an egg, in a nest. One day, the bird left to get some food, and while she was gone the egg began to crack. This baby bird poked its beak through the shell, then its head. The baby knew it was alone, so it hopped out of the nest, inched along the branch, and dropped itself onto the ground—it couldn't fly yet, Stella.

Not far down the sidewalk, the baby bird met up with a wiry, black dog. "Are you my mother?" asked the baby bird. "No I am not," said the dog.

It couldn't fly, but it could talk?

It's a story. Get out of your head, Stella. I don't have to tell it.

Okay. Okay. It could talk.

The talking bird was determined and continued down the street, asking a cat, a toy dinosaur, and a mitten if they were its mother. Each of them said no. The baby bird persevered and found itself at the edge of a construction site where a giant, yellow digging machine was parked. The baby bird climbed onto the giant teeth of the creature and shouted: "Mother, Mother, I found you." But the machine let out a snort from its exhaust. "You are not my mother. You are a snorty thing," said the baby bird who had now become trapped in the digger's massive bucket that was rising from the ground. "I want my mother."

Aurora, I want my mother.

I know you do, Stella. Shush.

The baby bird began to cry. And at that moment, the baby bird saw the branches of the tree, and just as the nest came into view, the snort dropped the baby back into the nest next to its mother.

The end.

Are you sleeping?

No, I was listening. And thinking. Are you my mother?

I'm your friend.

I don't think so, Aurora. I think you're my mother.

Okay, fine. Then you have to be my mother tomorrow.

I will Aurora, I will. I'll find a good story. And I'll even braid your hair.

I want my mother too. Stella. Why did I choose this stupid story?

Nova

When you mumble I can't hear you. Are you crying?

I was thinking about the stars. And our names. And the story. And our stories.

I never really knew her. I know you've heard me ask this a hundred times, but why does someone walk out when their kid is two? And why did she have to die? Where would I have lived if it wasn't for my grandpa? How can I want my mother?

What if the dog and the dinosaur and the mitten and the machine were wrong? What if everything is a mother?

You're crazy, Aurora.

What if we're each other's mother? What if we are each our own mother? What if a mother is bigger than just a person who disappears when you're little, or who's there but not there like you need her to be?

Tricia Jacobson

Aurora, stop.

No. Not stop. Go. Let's find out.

*The story is based on the book *Are You My Mother* by P.D. Eastman

2. QUESTLISTING AND CAMPING

Aurora, wake up. I found something over by the concession.

It's still dark.

I couldn't sleep. You said, "Let's go find out." About our mothers and who mothers are.

It was a metaphor, Stella. Not genealogy. I meant like go on a quest to find out the answers to what we're missing. To find guides, lessons, a kind of pilgrimage.

I'm not an idiot. I know you meant a metaphor—what you said was a symbol of what you meant. But I couldn't sleep so I went for a walkabout.

A walkabout? We're not in Australia.

Okay, I went over by the concession, in case it was left open. Just in case. And I wouldn't have taken anything more than a bag of chips, I really wouldn't. And all that talk last night made it hard to sleep. We're on this student camp-in-the-city thing, but really, you made it into something else last night. And, I found...

Please tell me it wasn't open.

There's a motion light. It comes on in the dark when a person is by the concession entrance.

I'm not eating stolen food.

Stop. I didn't go in. Okay, it was locked. But I found this list. Will you at least sit up? The sun's rising. I've never been up for one before and I know you haven't either. You've got to see this. I think it's a sign.

It looks like a list, not a sign.

Nova

You know what I mean. It's a piece of somebody's research paper. Look, you can just see a faded University of... along the top.

Stop pulling my sleeping bag. I'm not getting up yet. I'm warning you.

Aurora, this is important. You need to see this list. I've got this feeling.

There. Happy. I'm sitting, but I'm staying in my sleeping bag.

Read it. Read it aloud, Aurora.

It's too dark.

Squidge your body around so the rising sun's behind you. Hold the paper over a bit. You'll be able to read it.

"Necessary for Life." Stella, this is lame.

Read some more or I swear I'll pull you out of your sleeping bag. Look at the top! It says "The Quest."

No, Stella, it's torn. It probably said "The Questions."

No, don't you see? It says "The Quest." Maybe it was questions for some student who was studying, but it was by the concession for me to find, and it now says "The Quest." Keep reading.

"Needs… not wants…
"Faith
"Confidence
"Positive self-talk
"Positive body image
"To express gratitude
"A passion
"To be kind
"Air
"Water
"Food"

See, an amazing list, huh?

Nova

There's a quote on the other side.

"Once I had asked God for one or two extra inches in height, but instead he made me as tall as the sky, so high that I could not measure myself."

Okay, Aurora, that blew my mind a little bit. Did you just make that up?

As tall as the sky. Can you imagine being as tall as the sky. If you only asked for a couple of inches and you got more?

What about as tall as the stars? I want to be as tall as the stars.

Stella, we are the stars.

Whatever student's paper this is they sure are smart.

The quote is not your mystery student's. I've read it before. There was a girl on the other side of the world. I remember on the news. She was shot because she chose to go to school. Because she wanted to learn. Let me think... Malala Yousafzai. She wrote a book. *I Am Malala: The Girl Who Stood Up for Education* and Was Shot by the Taliban. She won a peace prize. I've seen her on TV since then. Looks like whoever wrote these notes had looked up Malala's work.

She was shot for wanting to go to school?

Can you imagine? There are places without basic freedoms.

I never learned anything useful from going to school.

We haven't learned *everything* useful from going to school.

There's a difference?

Of about four letters.

A-n-ything e-v-e-rything?

Nova

You learned numbers and letters at school, Stella. It's just that there's so much more. That's why we're doing this camping thing. To explore.

We're doing this because it's free. And it gets me away from Grandpa and you away from a foster home. And we got these cool sleeping bags and gear. But... But there's more, right?

Stella, why don't you watch the rest of the sunrise with your treasure, and I'll go back to sleep, and then we'll talk about it.

You mean you think it means something that I found it?

I think you have a wild imagination and some university student did some kind of study and lost some of their notes.

You know what? Even though you're the one that started "we're on a quest" thing, you go back to sleep. I am gonna watch the rest of the sunrise. I'll take my treasure, and I'm gonna ask for a sign.

Can you do it quietly?

You know what? I don't even have to ask. It has already happened. This list is the sign. And I'm gonna be the keeper of it.

My hair feels hot.

If you turn around you'll see why. The sky behind you is on fire. It lit up like that the second I took the paper from you.

The sky cannot be on fire.

Why not? The sun is a fireball.

When did you get all smarty-pants?

Take a look for yourself. You tell me if you've ever seen a sky that color. I've only seen those oranges and reds in flames. And your hair.

Okay, that is pretty amazing.

It's more than amazing. It's magnificent. What's that word for learning material that's prepared by a teacher for each grade?

Shhh, Stella. I'm watching the sunrise.

Thought you were sleeping in.

Impossible now. Curriculum.

Yeah, that's the word. Well this is our curriculum. This is what we're meant to learn.

"Faith
"Confidence
"Positive self-talk.
"Positive body image
"To express gratitude
"A passion
"To be kind
"Air
"Water
"Food"

We can't learn air, water, or food.

You said we were on a quest. This list shows up. Stop fighting it. We can learn about these things. This paper is a guide.

That paper was a poorly aimed throw at the garbage at the concession.

Aurora. I'll make a deal, let's drop the air, water, and food, and halve the list. Make what's left our curriculum. Pleeeeeeaaaase. We need a guide. The sign, the sun, the stars, this camping thing my grandpa said to go for, this space that's been given to us to sleep at night and explore during the day... summer camp for the messed up and poor.

Don't say that. That's on the list… already negative talk.

I was joking.

It's easy to dis ourselves by saying it was meant to be funny.

Please, Aurora, please. I feel this.

Faith, confidence, positive self-talk and body image, gratitude, kindness. How's that? Deal?

Deal if we can call it Questlisting our lives.

Oh, Stella, you're exhausting.

Oh, Aurora, you know you love me.

3. AURORA AND THE TREE

Hello, Aurora.

Who said that? Stella, are you back? Are you making a funny voice?

No, I'm not Stella. Stella went downtown, remember? Look up. That's right. Check out my maze of branches, twigs, and leaves.

You're a tree.

I know. You're sitting under me.

Do you want me to move?

No. I want to ask what you're reading.

An old favorite, *Anne of Green Gables*, while I wait for my friend.

Are those your sleeping bags?

Yep. We're on a quest.

You and Stella?

Yeah.

What kind of quest?

It's too hard to explain. I'll sound stupid.

You're talking to a tree.

That's true. Okay, so there's this kids' story about a bird trying to find its mother.

Oh, I know that one. That bird's nest was just up here on the branch I'm shaking.

You're making that up now. That's just the wind shaking your branch. Stella makes up things too; says things are bigger than they are. Sometimes, she says she did things when I know she didn't. And sometimes she says she didn't do things when I am pretty sure she did.

I'm not making it up. I know that bird. The yellow digger brought that baby bird back.

That's right.

So, Aurora, ask me that question you just thought about that you never thought you'd ask a tree, until it spoke to you.

I can't.

C'mon ask me. You're on a quest.

Are you my mother?

All mothers know their children's names, Aurora.

Not all mothers know their children, though, Tree.

I know you. When you were born, ribbons of light appeared in the night sky, a magnificent display called the northern lights… the aurora borealis. When you turn your head, I can still see those streamers in the glow of gold, orange, and red in your hair.

I know why that book's your favorite—Anne of Green Gables. *A made-up character, an orphan, who has the same features as you, a face speckled with freckles, constellations of them. She was as determined as you are. Sent to the Cuthbert's, a brother and sister who had sent for a boy to help them with their farm, she convinced them to keep her. She's not unlike you. Except she is a character, and you are real.*

That baby bird is a character, but you said the nest was in the tree.

Can I remind you you're talking to a tree?

Stella should be here by now. We both ran out of data so we can't text each other. We're basically offline. Dead to the world.

Aurora, open your book.

Hey, you changed the words. Where are my *Anne of Green Gables* pages?

I wrote something for you. Besides, I need to look for Stella. Read, Aurora. Read.

You know what Stella looks like? You know her?

All mothers know their children.

THE PAGES THAT TREE CHANGED

IDENTITY

You see all these trees around us? Not one of us identical. If you squint and tilt your head to the right, the trunk of that one over there looks like a dancing bear. The one next to it is completely twisted, gnarled like wisdom itself. I'm straighter and don't have as many marks on my trunk, and I'm taller. If trouble was headed our way, I'd see it first and call out to the others. We're all unique. None of us point to another and say, "Hey, you don't fit in."

Society is not like a forest. Society, through the beauty industry and a hunger for making money, has set ridiculous standards for us to believe we have to look a certain way. Social media and magazines push unrealistic images and saturate us with buy-this and fix-that messages: perfect teeth, glowing skin, video touch-ups. The selfie is not a selfie at all, it's a "me-as-I-choose-to-be-viewed-fie," an edited image. Fake.

The opposite of fake is real. The opposite of lie is truth. The opposite of phony is authentic. The secret of true beauty likes in authenticity—truthfulness. Full of truth. Not full of lie.

And being authentic used to come naturally. Now, it must be relearned.

Know this: the key to happiness is to live your truth. To be unapologetically yourself. Think about Anne Shirley of Green Gables. It's challenging to be truly authentic. To be yourself. It means going against the grain, knowing when to speak up. Understanding a set of natural rules within your heart and soul. These are your core values. It takes strength to be authentic.

Heal Your Past, Change Your Future

Can you remember when you were two? That was the first foster home you went to. It would be hard to remember before that, but you can remember by a way that you have been told your history from community helpers. And you can imagine some of it from the few photos that are around of the woman that a social worker called your tummy mummy. Later, you knew that meant your biological mother, even though you saw on documents that your legal guardian was filled out as "Ward of the State."

There have been more than a few foster homes, temporary placements, and a couple of hopeful forever homes. Through reading, you had a taste of what the character, Anne Shirley, experienced. Your neighbor, Miss Frankie, the wonderful older lady you helped when you were at your longest placement, gave you that taste. She planted the seeds for you to feel safe and share your feelings by sharing some of her own story. You could see she had a happily ever after. You dared to believe you could too.

She used to lean on me and read her books here too. Surprise, there are no coincidences, we're all connected.

Miss Frankie wasn't always an old lady living in a house full of trinkets, who sat in a rocking chair on her porch while a pumpkin pie baked in the oven. And, oh, how she enjoyed you coming over for a slice of it. When she was younger, the world almost lost her; she believed she was not beautiful enough.

Miss Frankie shared with you that she had a difficult time growing up. She left out the part where she was a model. What the world would call a famous model. Discovered when she was barely a teenager, she was thrust into a world that was inauthentic. She traveled all over the world on photo shoots. After a time, she started to speak out about the dangers of that life, the risks she was exposed to, and the vulnerability she felt. When she pushed for changes to some of the insane practices that her managers and handlers demanded, she was bullied, pushed away by those who she thought were her friends, and even threatened. She had no idea who she was anymore. That's when I met her. She'd come here. She'd sit under my branches. We'd talk.

When we are unapologetically ourselves, we are often cut off or put down by others. When we don't "agree" or "conform" with certain standards, when we question them, we can lose friends.

The loneliness of friendlessness is painful. We often think there is something wrong with us.

True friends lift their friends and listen, instead of

tearing them down if they don't conform—meaning go along with things you're not that comfortable with.

True beauty is confidence, courage, and kindness. If you ever find yourself feeling you have to say sorry for who you are, then you are with the wrong people, in the wrong place, or you are not in your true heart.

Aurora Interrupts:

Wait a minute, confidence and kindness is on Stella's Questlist. Do you have something to do with that? Or her finding it? But it does make sense. There is so much pressure to be a certain way, look a certain way... who makes up this stuff? Advertising? People who want to tell other people how to feel and what to buy? What does that have to do with friendship? Is all that pressure from companies that sell stuff affecting our relationships with other people? Is all that stuff covering up who we really are underneath all the brand names and labels? Are you listening, Tree? Or are you looking for Stella? I'll keep reading.

Danger Signs

If you find yourself replaying conversations and wondering if you should have said something different or differently, that is a sign that you're worried about fitting in and might do whatever is asked of you just to stay in "a group." Another is if you wonder what others are saying about you or thinking about you. Those are signs that you want to fit in or be accepted and may even depend upon being accepted. That's okay to a point, lots of humans do it—interestingly, dogs don't, cats don't, trees don't either. Everyone wants to belong. But sometimes we want it so badly that we start to hang with people we like, and then we do things and say things to get their approval. We overvalue their messages and undervalue our own values. We stop speaking our truth.

The idea of being brave enough to be the real you is a huge thing because that is the key to self-love. And once you love yourself, you never turn back. That's what Miss Frankie learned. And I know that is what you're learning.

And that's what Stella needs to learn.

Stella is surviving. You are a survivor who is learning to thrive. And Miss Frankie… well you know how well she did; she learned to thrive.

Those with the deepest relationships on earth are those who embrace who they are and understand that there is not one other person in the sea of over seven billion people on this planet who is exactly like them. You were designed to be the very person you are, and you were put on this earth to serve an incredible purpose. I want to help you understand your purpose, that's why I'm looking for Stella while you're reading the words I magicked on this page.

Mothers help others find their purpose. Mothers magic words on pages.

Hey, Tree? Are you back? Are you Miss Frankie's mother? Are you Stella's mother?

Star light, star bright, Aurora, I am the mother of authenticity. Keep reading.

TREE'S CONTINUED PAGES

What Other People Think is None of *Your* Business

It's important for your mental health to understand the importance of not worrying about the opinions of others, to learn to respond rather than react to some of the hateful words some use. Sometimes that response will be to ignore, other times it will be important to take calculated action. In these days of social media platforms, opinions and hurtful statements are thrown around like candy. These kinds of comments are not asked for but given anyway. It's horrible when people do it online because there's a twisted kind of freedom when the person isn't in the same room.

Being accepted is part of being human, but the quicker you understand how this desire to be accepted can lead to toxicity, the quicker you will understand that what others think about you is none of your business.

This is the why we need to be unapologetically ourselves. Why it's totally fine for me to be the tree I am and that tree over there to be who she is. It makes the world a more diverse place—the more diversity (variety), the more ideas, the more joy, the more thriving, the more solutions. It's vital to thriving that we be unapologetically ourselves. If we are not, we lose ourselves, and the world loses us on its pages.

Miss Frankie called this social courage.

If Miss Frankie had let the opinions of others persuade her to go against her own value system, you may never have eaten that pie, or found out how precious you are. Miss Frankie challenged the world she was in, then left the world of lies when she was still young.

Later, when Miss Frankie had a family, her three-year-old daughter insisted on wearing boys' clothes because they better fit her personality. Her daughter, Charlie, was confident, competitive, and athletic, often playing with boys at daycare. She grew up loving sports and adventures and playing in the mud. This brought with it the opinions of others.

"Why would you let your daughter wear boy clothes?"

"What kind of parent are you to let a young child make a decision like that?"

"You should force her to wear girls' clothes."

Miss Frankie thought the questions were ridiculous. The negative comments did not deter her from honoring her daughter's wishes. Miss Frankie had another idea. She thought rather than shop for her daughter's clothes in the boys' section, she'd start a line of clothing tailored for spirited girls. She had confidence in her decision, and she followed through. *The Huffington Post* published a story on Miss Frankie, her daughter, and the clothing line. Overnight, it seemed everyone was talking about the concept. But not all that talk was positive.

As the orders flooded in from all over the world, so did the comments and emails. Miss Frankie was excited to read them, expecting everyone to love the idea of clothing without the typical pinks and flowers. But in every hundred positives there were some ugly notes that were filled with hateful words. They gutted Miss Frankie. She found it hard to believe people would say such things. She remembered the strength she had gathered when she'd spoken up in the modeling community, and how she'd moved forward after she left it.

She refused to accept that negativity into her life. She chose to keep doing what she knew was of value. It led her to doing more to advocate for free-spirited girls. And you are proof. You've tasted her pie and enjoyed her brand of hospitality.

When you follow your truth, you move toward your purpose in life. That is when you are led to magnificent experiences. That is when the world grows. Wait, that is when you grow the world. That is when you grow.

There will be people who try to knock you down. They will try to devalue your ideas. Listen only to the constructive feedback (your heart will know what that is), and of the hurtful, unkind opinions: do not apply any value to them. It will hold you back from what you want and need to accomplish. You were put on this earth for a purpose. Even discovering a purpose is a purpose, for a while—an important step. Don't let someone else destroy your journey. The world needs your social courage.

Miss Frankie followed her heart. She refused to be taken in by peer pressure. Miss Frankie became a role model to more than just her children.

"Trees are like mothers.
They quietly drive important functions
that make all life possible in the
surrounding ecosystem."
Meg Lowman, aka Canopy Meg

Stella, you were gone ages.

There was an accident, and I stuck around to help. Hero and all, you know me. I've got us a pizza. And picked up a lip balm and some hair ties. Let's organize our camp site. We can sleep under the stars again.

What kind of an accident was it?

Whoa, this Hawaiian is great, huh? I love pineapple.

I talked to that tree today, over there.

That's cool.

And it talked to me.

Okay, that's weird. This is supposed to be a secure campground. Maybe we made a mistake coming here.

Stella, where was the accident?

I remember a story about a tree... and it's my turn to be Mother.

Nova

Did you get into trouble? Did you lift the balm and the hair stuff?

Hey! You're the one who had a conversation with a tree. You're the nut job here. Now do you want the story or not?

I want the story.

How many stars you figure up there tonight?

You asked me that last night.

A million?

As many stars as there have ever been children.

Aurora? Stay away from that tree. It's creepy looking.

No, Stella. It's beautiful. Truly beautiful. Full of truth.

Get comfortable, Aurora. Here's the story.

There was this apple tree and a boy who loved to climb it and eat its apples. The tree was a giving tree, and the boy and the tree spent lots of time together. The boy loved the tree. And the tree was happy. And the boy carved a heart at the bottom of the trunk with Me + T inside the heart.

When the boy became a teenager, he spent less time with the tree. One day when he came, the tree invited the boy to climb up and play, the boy said he was a teenager now and wanted to get some things and so he needed money. The tree told him it didn't have money, but it did have apples that he could take and sell, then he could get the things he wanted. And so the boy did.

When he visited again, he brought a lady with him. He carved another heart into the trunk and wrote Me + Y.L. inside the heart.

The tree continued to call the young man a boy and kept on giving. When the boy who was a young man wanted to build a house, the tree said to take its branches from above to build the house. And the boy that was now a man did. And the tree was happy.

The boy returned years later and said he needed a boat to sail away in. The tree said he should take the trunk, the whole trunk, chopping the tree to the ground, and make his boat. And the boy who was a man did. And the tree was happy.

When only the stump remained, with Me + T in a heart, the tree remained for many years without the boy, and without the carefree love of a little boy who used to climb all over and swing from branches that no longer existed. The tree was lonely. The tree was not happy.

Then the boy returned, a tired, old man. The tree explained there was nothing left to give. No shade, no branches to swing on, no apples to eat, no lumber for building materials, not even a trunk. The boy shared that his teeth were too weak for apples, he was too old and weak to climb, and all he wanted was a quiet place to sit.

The tree offered the stump. The old man, who the tree still called a boy, sat. And the tree was happy. The end. Are you asleep, Aurora?

He was kind of a taker from the tree, huh Stel?

I guess, but the tree was always happy to give.

Do you think it was really a tree, or do you think that was his mother?

I saw the pictures. When I was a kid. Simple drawings. It was a tree. They weren't related.

But pictures can mean other things. They can be symbols.

You're pretty smart.

Did the tree know the boy's name?

I don't remember.

I bet the tree knew the boy's name. All mothers know their children's names.

Now I wish I could remember. I'm such a loser. But I do remember the author drew the pictures too. And lots of people saw all kinds of meanings in that story. The man who wrote it was creative, like you. Give me a moment. I'm gonna remember his name. Shel Silverstein. There was a whole shelf of his books at school. I'm gonna go to a library and find them sometime.

Let's just say the tree did know the boy's name. It had to. And you're not a loser. You told a good story.

Wait! Aurora! What if the tree was Mother Nature and the boy was like all the people who cut down forests or drain lakes or just generally wreck nature?

I don't know. The message could have been how some people say we have to love all people and give to those who don't have.

But he was still a taker and took advantage. At least that's what I think.

It would be hard to be friends with someone who always took, if you were always giving. Not really an equal friendship.

I hope I'm not like that?

You're not, Stella. We're sharing the storytelling. Taking turns. We're giving and receiving. It's not even taking. We're listening to each other. We're letting ourselves be us. If there's anything you want to tell me, I won't judge you. I want you to be unapologetically you. Socially courageous.

You're too deep. How about we leave it at BFF?

Yes, best friends forever.

Hey, we forgot to Questlist.

Forgot to what?

Nova

I don't want to mess up on the first day.

The first day of what? It's almost the middle of the night.

Just say check after each one. I memorized them today.

Check what?

I'll show you.

Confidence. Check. I didn't feel scared when I told you about the list this morning. Positive self-talk. Check. I told myself I could learn from this list. Body image. Check. Sort of. I didn't compare myself to any pictures on social media... but then, I have no data and my battery's dead. Gratitude. Check. Tonight when I slid inside this sleeping bag I had a little flash of thank you to Mountain Equipment for donating these to us losers. Whoops, fail now on the pst.

The pst?

The positive self-talk. I called myself a loser.

What about the faith?

I don't know. I am not a churcher. Grandpa is. I can't do a check about the faith.

Faith. Uncheck. Neither of us know what it is.

No, It's not that. I think I know what faith is. I think we all do. I just don't know if I did anything to believe in something larger than myself today.

And kindness. Check or uncheck?

I can't do the whole list every day.

You said hello to the people who run this place. I saw you when I was under the tree.

That's not kindness, is it? That's just normal.

Nova

Stella. Kindness. Check. You said hello to someone. I saw them smile.

"Sometimes I like to listen to Ariana Grande, and cry about all the farm animals who think they're family until the day they're betrayed and become food."

Okay that's just weird. You think that? Or you heard it?

I read it on the internet. I just remembered it.

What do you think it means? Like what was the context?

I don't think we always have to know the meaning of stuff. It can just be stuff that makes us feel.

I like order. I like solved mysteries. I like constellations so I can form patterns of the stars and not just have them all out there random-like and scattered.

Do you think Ariana Grande grew up on a farm?

I worry about you sometimes, Stella. I think you might have to add one more category to your Questlist. Insanity. Check.

I'd rather call it being me. Not saying sorry for who I am.

You mean being unapologetically you?

That describes it exactly.

You been reading my book?

Aurora, now who's lost it? You know I don't read books.

4. STELLA AND THE SPOON

Rise and shine!

Stella, what's happening to you?

If we roll up our gear and stash it with the women in the park concession, we could go to IHOP for breakfast. I checked in with my grandpa yesterday. He gave me a twenty.

You didn't buy a phone card for your cell?

A girl's gotta eat.

A girl's gotta text. Especially when that girl is you.

Think of it as an electronic detox.

When did you get all balanced and forward-thinking?

When I wanted pancakes more than data.

How was your grandpa?

He was cool. You know... he tries to fill in for my mom. Asked about you. I told him you're keeping me on the good side of the tracks. He's cool with the quest, especially since this is a designated safe area for seasonal campers and there are people who live here full time and manage it. Says he thinks of us as being at summer camp; told me when he was a boy, he rode train cars across some state to a place I never heard of.

He's trying his best, Stella.

He asks me the same thing. Did you visit your mamma's grave? Are you brushing your teeth? And he's added one thing. He said when we're done if you want to stay with us instead of going where the social worker says he's cool with that.

He likes the word cool.

He does his best.

Pancakes?

Oh, yeah.

Thank you, Grandpa Brown.

Maple syrup is so much better than a phone.

For now. But what about later, when our stomachs are full, and our inboxes are unavailable?

I wish I could take a selfie with this pancake. It's as big as my face.

You don't need data to do that, Stella.

I know. I just need to plug in the phone somewhere. Besides, who would I send it to? I have no data. I have no friends.

You may not have data, but you know lots of people. The picture could be for yourself. We need to get the cords from the bottom of the knapsack and find a place to plug in. That pancake is worthy of its own selfie.

Did you ever notice the washroom door sign for women looks like a cape, not a dress?

I saw that meme on Facebook.

It's right there on the door, in real life. Look. And did you ever notice the clean and organized way these napkins come out of the dispenser? Or when you look at yourself in a spoon, your face is super tiny on one side, and the other side, the scoopy part, you're upside down?

Nova

What, are we playing a notice game now?

Well, we don't have Candy Crush do we? Aurora! Play this game. It's in the now. It's fun.

Did you ever notice we use both hands to eat when we don't have our phones?

Look at them all.

The people?

The phones. They're everywhere.

Hey, look me in the eyes. Yeah, like that but not so spooky. Did you ever notice people don't look at each other when they eat. Crapola, Aurora, we're having a conversation without electronics. Knife. Fork. Syrup. Eye contact.

If you did a selfie now, with the pancake as big as your face, now that would be real. Untouched. Not a societal demand for perfection.

Let me guess, more wisdom from that tree?

Look, it's even got a nose and ears. But if you did that, even that kind of selfie, the world would think you were all IHOP breakfast happy.

I am all IHOP breakfast happy.

But the people seeing the selfie would think you IHOPpy-happy all the time. You're not. Most posted pictures are only snippets of life. Why are we compelled to do it? Like when do people ever post the crap side of life?

We are on the crap side of life.

That's my point. Yet before our phones ran out of data. Before the contracts ran out and we bought phone cards like poor people do, we posted stuff that made our lives look amazing.

You're freaking me out again. Don't bring down my relationship with this cinnamon toast, okay? And a lot of budget-conscious people buy phone cards.

Nova

It reminds me of Miss Frankie.

The old lady with the pumpkin pie?

Yes. No, she's not an old lady. She was a model. She lived in the false world for a while.

Go for it. There's no stopping you now. Just explain it to me like I'm six. I don't have the energy to listen to any high-end lecture.

The point is that what we see on social media isn't real. At least it isn't the whole truth. Most of the friends, family, and influencers we follow only show the good. They don't always let you into the bad, the struggles, the images of them with no makeup. They don't necessarily talk about the hoops they've had to jump through or the hurdles they've had to overcome. They don't always share the raw truth: maybe they sometimes feel inadequate, anxious, or depressed.

It's not that people should be obligated to show the less-than-perfect parts of their lives. That's not the point. The point is to be sure we don't get sucked into thinking their lives are better than ours. Or get trapped into believing their lives are perfect. They are not. Everyone struggles. Everyone is battling something they don't expose on social media. This is just a part of life.

I think if we can get our contracts going again, like if we get part time jobs, or even are able to buy a phone card, it'll be great. We don't have to dump social media, but I've got this feeling that this forced detox is... erm... I can't think of the phrase, but it is teaching us something.

Knowledge is power.

You were listening. That's exactly it. Are you sure you haven't talked to Tree or read the Anne book?

You give me too much credit. Knowledge is power. It says it here on this little newsy-letter printout between the salt and pepper shakers.

But you are right, Stella, knowledge is power. We just learned by playing your noticing game how much power is taken away from us when we are attached to our phones. Or attached to the lifestyle that attaches us to the phones.

Make sure that social media is a tool you use—not a tool that uses you.

Does it say that on that newsletter-ey thing too?

No. I just said that. Made it up myself. See, I do listen to you.

Hey. Your Questioninglist thing?

Questlisting.

Right. Well. Confidence. Check.

How so?

Because our conversations are growing us. Growing us up. And that builds confidence.

As tall as the sky?

Not yet. One day. Maybe.

Can you believe it? The IHOP manager said we were the first real people she'd seen in forever. Our breakfast was on the house. We can spend the twenty on a phone card.

But that's how we ended up with a free meal. Because we weren't using our phones.

I feel like our conversations make me a dog chasing its tail.

Woof, woof.

No, really, Aurora. Chasing my tail is a good thing. I feel our life is getting serious. This really is a quest, isn't it? We thought it was just taking off,

Nova

getting away from your social worker, me taking a break from Grandpa, and now look at us. We just got called out in a good way, for being real. Isn't that amazing?

It would have been if you hadn't taken the fork and extra jams.

They'll never miss them.

That's not the point.

I'll take the fork back, but I'm keeping the packets of jam.

That works for me.

What's happening to us?

Something, for sure. I don't know what. But I know I can't go back to who I was yesterday or the day before. I need to go on my hero's journey.

Your what?

I've heard about it before. Something about discovering yourself. There's a story about a golden Buddha. I'll try to remember it. Tell you tonight. Let's get our stuff from the concession and set up our spot again. We have the whole week for free on our student pass, and free bottled water, and showers. And twenty dollars.

And a fistful of jam. (And a magic mirror spoon.)

I'll wait here while you return the fork.

5. AURORA AND STELLA DIG FOR GOLD

Aurora, you're not going to believe it. The campground hosts, you know that guy with the long beard and his grandma-lady wife who doesn't wear a bra, who stay in their trailer and run the concession and stack and sell the firewood and check people in? The ones you saw me say hello to?

Stewards.

No, not the Stewarts. Her name's Pinky and his name is Owl.

Campground hosts are called stewards.

Well, la-de-da know-it-all. They're Pinky and Owl, and I don't know their last name. Well, Pinky asked us to fill in for a couple of hours tonight and tomorrow night at the concession. She'll pay us seven dollars an hour each, cash, and we get to keep whatever sandwiches are two days old. And we can fill up a re-useable cup from the soda fountain while we're there. Bottomless iced tea.

And you said yes? For both of us?

Well, duh. She wants us to show at six for a bit of training, and she'll be gone by seven, and we'll lock up at nine. Owl will be in the trailer or doing his rounds if we have anything major happen.

Stella, how does she know we're trustworthy?

Are you trustworthy?

Oh, please. Of course I am.

Then she can trust us.

Nova

There'll be money changing hands, Stella.

Can you count? I can.

Stella, I'm not even tired. I love the awesome teamwork when we lined up all those buns.

Three egg salad sandwiches, two ham, for us to eat after you take the key and cash to Owl. I'm so full of iced tea I gotta pee. Oh, Aurora, it wasn't even like a job. I didn't even mind wiping the counter. I felt... I felt... wanted.

And we still get to sleep under the stars.

Let's eat the egg when you get back from handing over the money and key. Ham in the morning for breakfast?

Maybe we can get some firewood tomorrow and have a fire at night, and some marshmallows.

You mean after our shift?

Oh right. Tomorrow night we should plug our phones in while we work. We'll have a camera and a clock even without data or Wi-Fi.

Hurry up and go see Owl. Then we can eat. Then it's story time, you promised that story about the golden hoodie.

Golden Buddha.

Go, Aurora. I'm hungry. I didn't eat a single thing when we were in there. I'm so fricking proud of myself.

Do not ask me how many stars are up there.

Do you think Pinky makes the egg sandwiches in her trailer and brings them in? There's no official label.

Nova

They were magic. I'm full. And I'm warm. And I love being out here with you.

Are you all tucked in? Like you can't easily slide out of your sleeping bag to reach me?

Totally zipped in. Why?

How many stars do you think are up there?

The only reason I'm going to tell you this story, Stella, is because I want to hear it myself. Otherwise, since I can't get out of my bag and swat you, I would hold the story back.

You are so funny.

You're the one that should do standup, Stel.

C'mon. My eyes are already closed. Once upon...

Once upon a long, long time ago, like more than six hundred years ago, in a far east country called

Thailand, there was a golden statue of a dude the people of Thailand worshipped. His name was Buddha. The statue was almost ten feet tall and weighed over ten thousand pounds. It would be worth hundreds of millions of dollars today.

That could be more dollars than stars.

Stella, are you listening?

I thought you were only telling it for yourself.

Three hundred years after it was built, the Buddhist people discovered an army was going to invade their country. They knew they would be annihilated because they were a peaceful people and did not fight. They quickly began covering their statue with plaster and muddy clay and even some bits of glass, so it looked quite dull and boring. They hoped that when the invaders came through, they would not find their beloved statue.

During the invasion, all non-fighting people were murdered by the warring people, but guess what?

They didn't even clue in that the statue was valuable?

Exactly.

But all the people were killed.

I know. That sucks. But the people of Thailand, the people that were peaceful and followed the Buddhist ways, moved back to that area many years later, and two hundred years after the invasion, they built a kind of retreat near the existing statue.

One day, when they were moving it—the statue… and it was hard to move, but it was 1957 so there was equipment—they noticed a crack in the clay.

This is where if this was a movie, there would be some kind of fantasmagorical harp music right?

That music would be amazing and match the shining of the gold through the crack.

Beyonce's tunes would work.

I had thought something more like Disney orchestral, you know like from videos we watched when we were little. Like Moana.

Or Ariana Grande.

Well, there wasn't any music, unless you count the beat of a little hammer. One of the people gently chipped away and eventually revealed that the whole statue was solid gold. Some of the elders then recalled the stories they'd been told by their grandparents, who had been told by their grandparents, that there had been such a statue.

That's it? Where's the wisdom? Where's the mother? Where's the talking tree who gives all of itself to a creepy, greedy kid? Tell me what I'm supposed to get by this story.

Well, here's what I was told by Miss Frankie. That inside of each of us lives a golden light. We are supposed to find it.

Nova

It'd be pretty hard to find mine. My whole life has been a daily mess, piling layer upon layer of clay and crap over my so-called goldenness.

Miss Frankie said something I didn't get, but now I might. She said the thickest layer of clay is what we put there ourselves. We cover ourselves up by not being open minded to things.

Well, that's probably right. But a lot of that is what we've learned by what others tell us is "the right way." You know, like you said about all the stuff we see online. And advertising from stores... wear these jeans and your life will be amazing.

I think when we learn to think for ourselves, then we start to take some of that clay off.

Hand me a hammer and chisel because I've got a lot to chip through to see if there's any gold under there. I'll start with my head, 'cause I know my thinking hasn't been all that great in my life. Got anything else from Miss Frankie before I start renovating?

I think we have started reconstruction, Stella. Seriously. Think about how deep our conversations have been since school's been out. Miss Frankie said to reconnect with things that brought us joy in our lives.

Good one. There go all my hopes at gold panning. I have nothing in the past.

That's not true. We have something really amazing in our past. Think back to grade four. First day of school. The swings.

That's the day we met.

And you have your grandpa. And he tries so hard to give you a good home.

And you have the time you spent with Miss Frankie. If it weren't for her, we wouldn't know there was gold in dem dar hills, pardner.

True. Now I'm going to sleep. I've got strawberry and whipped cream over a stack of flapjacks just behind my eyelids.

Nova

How does Zonda have thousands of followers on her makeup YouTube?

Go to sleep.

How does she manage it? Is she the kind of girl that goes on a quest?

She doesn't need to. She got a fancy convertible for her sixteenth birthday.

I bet it's gold.

It's red, and a two-seater. She can't fit all those followers in there.

She can on her devices. On her channel.

Think about what you'd cover in concrete and clay so others couldn't steal it.

I don't have anything valuable.

That's not true.

Tell me, Aurora. Tell me what that is.

Go to sleep.

Not before I questlist.

Again?

I'll be fast if you do one of them.

Stop bargaining with me.

Confidence. Check. I felt two inches taller when that concession job conversation came up. It was like Pinky and Owl saw something good in me and then I saw something good in me too. And knew that goodness was true. Negative self-talk. Uncheck. I know I just said a bunch of negative things about myself when you were telling the hoodie story.

Buddha.

Right. Boo-dah. Now you.

Faith. Check. Sort of. I have been thinking about how many belief systems are all around the world, and if they all land in one camp of goodness. I think I'm questing, Stel.

Hey, Aurora. I was just thinking about Zonda. I don't want to judge her, even though I did and I do and I might again. But seriously, I bet people who have everything: a mom, dad, nice house, and a car at sixteen, don't always feel like they have everything. Their parents could be at work all the time. Or closed to their children's ideas.

Or put too much pressure on their children.

We might not be the only ones looking for our mothers. I mean, we know where we're at. You're all foster home certified, and I'm all mother-dead, grandpa-had-to-raise-me. There are little kids and tweenies and young adults who are sitting in what we don't have, and they still don't have it. Reminded of it every day.

Money can't buy everything, can it?

But twenty bucks got us a pancake breakfast and then we ended up not having to pay.

UNABLE TO SLEEP, STELLA TRIES TO TALK TO TREE.

TREE WRITES TO STELLA

Hey, Tree. I know there's a curfew here. But I can't sleep, and Aurora is snoring, and she said you talk. Can you?

Hello, I said. Come on Ms. Tree. Talk to me.

Hey, don't be dropping your branches. Excuse me, that almost hit me. I want a voice. Like Aurora heard. Now you just dropped your sappy leaves and twigs on something.

It's Aurora's book. Anne of Green Gables. How'd it get here? It's always in her backpack. Did you steal it?

Nova

You know what? You can't talk any more than I can become some kind of young role model of the century, inventing a kind of place where kids can talk on a live show, and I can help them, and make a place where they can do their laundry, get a snack, feel safe, learn, chill, shower, spend time with their true selves. Holy crap, listen to me. Where did that come from? I'm outta here. And I'm returning the book you stole. And stop looking. It's not like I'm heading for the night lamp by the concession to read it. I'm not. I'm just going to check you didn't tear out any pages, you trunky thief.

Hello light at the concession. Don't speak to me. Like really, I couldn't take it. Just shine.

Hello spoon. How do you like your little home in my pocket? I know, I know. You're stolen property. Worse, I never told Aurora. But I need you because I need me. Let's see, where am I. Upside down on this side. That's better, I'm tiny but can see my whole face. Hello Stella. Hello me.

Spoon, I'm going to pretend you're a video cam like they have on those reality shows that are not reflections of real life. I'll film a Stella spoon cam.

I want to be real.

Look at me, tiny reflection on the back of a spoon.

I want to be real.

Is this real?

Today I felt a tiny shift.

I think it's the stories.

I think it's this quest.

I want my mother.

Are you my mother?

No, you are me on the back of a spoon.

Nova

Me.

On the back of a spoon.

That I stole.

Here's a promise.

I will return you when it is time.

I will know when it is time.

I may not feel real yet, but I know I am growing.

I. Am. Growing.

Today I laughed.

Today someone saw value in me and treated me to breakfast.

And that was after my grandpa also gave me the money for breakfast.

Then I laughed with Aurora and she told me I was funny.

Then Pinky asked us to work.

Four people saw value in me, spoon. Four people.

I am lovable.

Make that five.

Hey, when other things like tree and light don't talk to me, they help me talk. I could get used to this. If I grow up maybe I can do something with this.

STELLA OPENS THE MAGIC PAGES IN THE BOOK

Stella, I may not have spoken to you, but I showed you the book, and I put down these words for you to read under the light of a tiny shed that has become a concession that feeds people, provides a living for a couple named Pinky and Owl, and has drawn you into a story of your own.

Guess what? You are building a tribe. And that is a wonderful thing. Questlisting. Do you know how self-driven and clever that is?

Sometimes, people get lost in having a ton of friends. It seems to me that when there are large groups competing for attention, then those large groups can determine how you measure your happiness.

When you build a tribe. Naturally connect with others—and that can be done through social media too, but not only social media. You can do it through meeting people, volunteering, random bumping into others, one or two people in a class or course. All these people, you learn from them, and you teach others, and you become close. Those are the friends that will stand up for you. Those are the friends you will stand up for. They are your tribe, and you are theirs.

True friends lift you. Encourage you. Fight for you. They stand by you in good times and in bad. They forgive you. They ask for forgiveness. Even when there is drama, especially when there is drama, in the hallways of school and the threads on text messages, real friends step in.

Real friends do not: talk behind your back. Create drama. Take credit for things you have done.

Here's the magic. The real magic. More magical than the words on this page.

Choice.

You get to choose the people you spend time with. You don't have to rush into relationships. You don't have to stay in them. You can make mistakes. Some people are very good at disguising their motives.

You are as good as the people you surround yourself with. Choose wisely.

Oh, how will you know. Usually, if it doesn't feel right, it probably isn't.

While it's important not to overjudge, it is vital to trust your heart and let it meet with your brain so you can evaluate and navigate your relationships.

The light will go off in a few minutes. That is the light at the concession. The light will never dim in you. Hurry back to your sleeping bag. And… it's okay about the spoon. You are right. You need it right now. Use it. Not for soup, but for reflection and affirmation. Affirmation, you ask? That's what you did tonight when you said "I am…"

There are so many ways to communicate besides speaking.

Goodnight, Stella, my sweet daughter of the earth, with hair the color of fertile soil that grows delicious food, with a heart so big it can, and will, love the whole world.

6. PINKY ON DITCHING DRAMA

Aurora, wakey, wakey. Only one of the toilets is working. There's a water pipe problem underground. They've got a plumber coming. If you have to go, I'd go now. And, by the way, your tree friend is a thief. I've put your book in your knapsack. Is that coffee?

Pinky brought it to us. Extra large with cream. She likes you. She told me. She's coming back. Wants to talk to us.

Weird.

That she likes you, or that she's coming back?

Tricia Jacobson

PINKY'S VISIT

You girls are such a blessing. Refill? I've got donuts too. They'll go with those ham sandwiches. You were lucky there were a couple left. I cook the ham myself, so I'm glad it's not going to waste.

Thank you for taking care of the concession. I've got your pay right here.

And such manners. And no phones. What a change. I'm constantly being asked for the Wi-Fi code. We don't offer one. Our own is secured. This is a sanctuary in the city. Oh, sure there's signals for those who have data, but… enough about the internet. I'm more about the internal network of ourselves and our connections to each other. And you girls got me thinking.

I met one of my dearest friends in the seventh grade. We didn't know each other well, but she approached me one day and asked me to spend the night. I did, and from that day forward Nicole, aka Bones, and I became inseparable. We spent nearly every single day together that year, even going on vacation together. She got me to join the swim team, something we ended up doing together until we graduated high school. We created such a strong friendship, more like a sisterhood. The memories we created are some of my favorites. Her family became my family, and my family became hers.

One of my favorite memories with Nicole was Halloween night and we decided to TP her house, cover it in toilet paper, as a joke. It was something teens used to do back in my day. We were all dressed up in costumes and as we were TPing her house, her father came out not realizing it was us and sent her dogs out to get us. We were running as fast as we could from her barking dogs as they were chasing us, and we were yelling at her dad to stop them. Once her father and dogs realized it was us, we fell down in laughter. We laughed so hard that night because—who would have thought her dad would have sent her dogs after us?

All these years later, forty at least, we are still in touch even though we went our own ways, met other people. The friendship we have now is as sacred as the one we had when we were kids. Maybe more. Friendship is precious. And true friendship can be thousands of miles apart. I had other friends too; they came and went. Some were real and others were what they thought was real.

Now I want you girls to do something for me. I call it the having-the-courage-to-be-disliked bootcamp.

Open your hands and close your eyes. Now I am placing a key in your hand, Stella, and now one in your hand, Aurora. Okay, you can open your eyes. This isn't an actual key, but a metaphorical key. A key to happiness; the courage to be disliked.

I wish I had developed the courage to be disliked in my teen years because it would have saved me a lot of anxiety. I let a lot of people into my life because of peer pressure, and I alienated others too because I went along with the crowd.

I think when we're teens we don't stop and talk about meanness and self-centeredness enough. We create drama around it, or others do, and we get involved in that drama, but we don't look at the cause.

Here's the thing: sometimes people have issues that have nothing to do with you, but they take it out on you. Sometimes people have such deep insecurities and are so miserable that they want those around them to be miserable and insecure as well and sometimes this is translated into people not liking you. There are going to be situations in your life, as a teen and as an adult, when people dislike you for irrational reasons, reasons you had nothing to do with.

It's not really that people dislike you. It's that they are in circumstances that make it impossible to accept you.

This can happen at any age, between people who are supposed to be bound by family love. And that is okay. It doesn't feel okay always. But it is.

Once you learn to have the courage to be disliked, or not accepted, because you understand you can only be you and other people can only be them, then you can use the key I placed in each of your hands to open doors to happiness, to thriving, and you will be able to close the door on anxiety and worry.

What's important to remember is that when you dislike someone else, then that can be about you too. No one is perfect. Everyone is imperfectly perfect. That's what makes us who we are. Who would want to be happy all the time? How would they know what happiness was? Who would want a smooth, flat road all the time, when it's great to have a hill to climb, to discover a view from, and then slide down the other side?

There is a book written by Ichiro Kishimi and Fumitake Koga called, *The Courage to Be Disliked*. In it is a quote I want to share with you:

"If you want to fly, give up everything that weighs you down."

You see, if you allow others to weigh you down, you will never fly.

I would add to that, don't think of it as disliking you. Think of it as disliking themselves so that you are in their crossfire at that time in their lives. And take a long look at yourself, in times of distress, and ask yourself if you are likeable to yourself, by yourself.

In a world of billions of personalities, everyone belongs, but we do not have to choose to be with everyone or anyone, nor do they have to choose to be with us.

Now, I've gotta get going. There are some changes taking place in the park. Owl and I are rolling with them the best we can. We're doing what we can to stand up for the good, and we're always looking for solutions. He's a wise one, that Owl. Oh, I know… groan on the wise owl. It's silly. But it's so freeing to be silly sometimes.

Aurora, she's deep.

Do you think she wrote that list of questions that was torn and you made into Questlisting? She sure hit home about positive self-talk and body image.

What I heard was—the more you like yourself the free-er you are.

What I heard was the more you be yourself, the more you like yourself, the free-er you are.

I'll take your 'be yourself, like yourself, free-er' and add one more thing. She said without saying it that everything is connected. All the things on the Questlist, that she doesn't even know about, are connected: confidence, positive self-talk and body image, gratitude, kindness.

You missed faith.

No, I didn't. I inferred it. Faith is like the ribbon tied around the package of wonder and wonderful.

I didn't hear her say that.

No, I came up with that. I know faith is out there. I know it's something big and amazing and personal and all encompassing. I know we're going to find it.

That confident, are you?

You know I am.

Yes. I know you are. I believe. I feel it too. We're at some kind of tipping point.

Aurora, we're not going to tip. I won't let you fall. We're gonna soar.

Stella, who are you? I don't know you anymore.

I hardly recognize myself these last couple of days.

I wish she was the grandmother I never knew because of the mother I never knew. I'm sorry, Stella. She was supposed to lift us, and she did, with the coffee, donuts, and story. And I love what's happening to you… and even a little bit to me… but I just feel down today. And I feel worried. Like something sad is going to happen.

Maybe she is your grandmother. Maybe she's everyone's grandmother. Maybe something is about to happen. Maybe it's your intuition. Maybe we are going to have some choices to make.

7. AURORA THE ADVOCATE

I returned the coffee pot. Checked to see what time we need to be there for our shift. And I snagged us some firewood from a bunch of people who are leaving today. They gave it to us. I didn't steal it. Does that make you feel happier?

I'm restless, Stella. Like there's something stirring underground.

Maybe you're one of those freaks that can predict an earthquake. Like horses run around before a storm.

Horses run around before storms?

I need you to feel happier so I can tell you something that might fit your category of something's going to happen.

That sounds like a lead-in to bad news. What did you do?

There is a mark on the tree. It wasn't there before. Your special tree. Now don't get too upset. The mark is because it's going to be cut down. Apparently, it's too old and a threat to some pipes underground. There's a petition, I put our names on it, but Pinky says it's too late.

Nooooooooooooo.

Aurora, where are you going. Come back! All our stuff's here.

Okay, you're crazy. Are those the trailer chains from behind the concession? Are you still going to work your shift tonight?

I'm staying chained to Tree. It's too wise to cut down.

You can't fight them.

Who are they, anyway?

The people over there in high-visibility vests and hardhats with that giant yellow digger thing.

What a betrayal, that's the digger who put the baby bird in the nest.

You're delusional, Aurora. What's come over you? That was a kid's story about a bird. Remember, it spoke to a mitten. Look, Pinky is negotiating with them now because she knows you're attached to the tree. They don't want any press. They're packing up everything ready for tomorrow. Come on, see they're leaving for the day, unchain yourself.

Join me.

I can't.

You mean you won't.

It's not possible.

You are supposed to be my best friend.

I need to work for both of us. That's how I'm going to support you, you idiot.

Oh, Stella. I'm sorry. Don't go. I mean go to work tonight. But don't leave me.

I'm not. Settle down. Watch me be your freaking best friend.

Our shift is done. It wasn't that busy. Here's your sleeping bag. Here's a bottle of water. Two hot chocolates. Yes, I paid for them. Four sandwiches, two of them are tuna, the other two are mystery meat because Pinky didn't have time to cook a ham.

You're not staying? We're not eating together?

I have to go.

Nova

It's dark. Where are you going?

I'll be back. Just talk to your tree, drink your hot chocolate, ignore the gathering crowd of campers, and relax before the reporters show. Word is spreading. Pinky can't keep them out when daylight comes. This may be the last good night's sleep you get before fame.

Where are you going? Keep who out?

My grandpa always says when he went anywhere, going to see a man about a horse. Well, I'm going to see an activist about a tree.

THE TREE SPEAKS

Aurora, why can't you trust her?

How can you be all social-workery-speak when your own life is in danger?

Did I say my life was in danger? Besides, I'm pretty confident it isn't now that you're fighting for me.

I am one person. Over there is a digger the size of a convenience store. Tomorrow there'll be a whole crew of modern-day lumberjacks.

All you say is true. And that's okay.

She lies. I worry. Where could she be going this time of night?

No. You are lying. It's not worry.

I am not a liar. I worry about her. That's not a lie. Why are you being this way?

Because I want to hear you say it.

Say what? I've said it. She lies sometimes. I worry.

Nova

She's probably getting into trouble.

Trouble? You're the one chained to a tree.

So that you can give me a hard time.

Some people call it a hard time, others would say a lesson.

Fine. There's nothing else to do here but stay chained to you.

Why are you chained to me?

Because you have a right to be here. It's a park. You're a tree. They're not cutting down the dancing bear or the twisted whatever it is.

Shall I start it for you? You, Aurora, believe I have a right to be here. But don't you think that you deserve the same kindness, gesture, shall we say love, from a friend, as you give to others? I need you to say it so that we can turn this around by morning. I need you to find the gold inside you. And we don't have much time.

Come on. Finish this off...

No one needs to do anything for me because I am not....

I like doing things for others. I really do. There's nothing else but that.

I know you are good to others. There's no doubt about that. Now, don't go all silent. You can do this. You have to so we can reverse it.

Repeat after me: no one needs to do anything for me because I am not....

I don't need anyone to do anything for me because I am not needy.

You know that's not it. Please, work with me here. No one needs to anything for me because I am not...

Because I am not... worthy of having things done for me.

That wasn't so hard, was it? After all, that is what you wrongly believe.

Wrongly? I am *not* lovable. If I was lovable my mother wouldn't have left. I have no idea where she is. What she calls herself. Who does that to a child? How can I be worthy? If I was worth something she would have stayed. Stopped doing drugs. Stopped. Stopped. Stopped.

Don't stop. Let it out.

No. People will hear me. Someone will come if I cry.

That might be a good thing.

No, I only want to be with you.

And I am going to tell you that I must go, but I will not be gone.

Don't mess with my mind. These chains are heavy enough.

You can remove them.

I don't want to. Look, they're on me to protect you.

I didn't mean those chains.

Oh, for goodness sake, so many metaphors. I feel like I'm back in English class.

And what was wrong with that? You loved the stories.

Why do you always have to be right?

What if there are no wrong answers?

The lumberjacking freaks aren't right?

How do you know?

They're going to cut you down.

What if I'm ready to go? What if my roots have wrapped around pipes that bring people water? What if I'm tired?

Nova

What if I'm ready for whatever is next?

You're ready to be sawdust? Woodchips? A bathroom for hamsters? Listen, I know that story of the giving tree. You can't possibly be happy as a stump. Sawdust, woodchips, and stumps are dead. Aren't they?

Well, just so you're prepared, it's not a pretty picture, they'll grind the stump and put some systemic poison so that the roots curl away from the pipes so that people can get their drinking water.

You're saying you're martyring yourself so others will drink?

I'm saying that I'm ready to be another form.

Like an angel tree in tree heaven?

Maybe.

I'm not going to unchain myself.

No, not now. And that is good. You'll know when.

I can't believe you're just giving up.

You'll know when. Go to sleep. I need to say see ya later to the dancing bear tree and the rest of my children.

STELLA RETURNS

Aurora, wake up. This is Sam. He's an artist— a carpenter—and an activist. This is his partner, Magdalena. And their baby girl, Freedom.

Stella what are you talking about?

They started the petition. Now they have a proposition for the city. To preserve the tree in another way. They understand it is time it comes down, but they want to create a legacy, make benches from its wood for the park. So, get up. There's about a hundred people with their own chains who are going to join you until the council agrees to the plan. I'll take your place right now while you pee and shower. You're gonna have your picture taken a lot today.

Stella?

Go, go, go. You've got fifteen minutes.

WHISPERED

Aurora. Let go and let love. Let go and let legacy. It's all happening perfectly.

Stella, did you say something?

I said go with Magdalena. Why are you hearing voices again? I told you, that tree doesn't talk.

MAGDALENA ACCOMPANIES AURORA TO THE SHOWER BUILDING

Your friend is pretty amazing. She was relentless at tracking people down from the petition, finding us. And you, such a selfless act. What a team you make. What an impact.

It talks, you know. The tree.

They all do. Always have, always do. Even when they are transformed. Everything has a voice. Every 'thing' is not a thing. Even this door to the showers, even these clothes I brought you... this yellow summer dress and purple leggings. I'll tell you a story while you dress.

MAGDALENA'S STORY

You might think being kind is all about the person who receives the kindness. And while that is true, real kindness is a circle. The true benefactors of acts of kindness fall to the giver.

Nova

There are physical and emotional benefits to being kind, beyond changing lives. There have been official studies about it, but who needs those when the proof is there in the feeling and the ripple effect? But it's true. Universities have studied that performing acts of kindness, or even just watching and being aware of them, for seven days boosts moods—makes people feel fantastic. And most of all, brings connection.

Freedom is living proof of what kindness can do.

Sam and I weren't always close friends. All through school he would frustrate me, hanging by my locker and teasing me. He'd say such cruel things. I couldn't stand being near him, but we ended up in some of the same classes and the teacher always sat us together. I've always said it was God's way of teaching me patience and, ultimately, kindness.

My grandparents lived next door to my family, and I confided in my grandmother about my frustration with Sam. Every time I'd head to school, she'd say, "Cover him in kindness, Maggie."

Grandma's words gave me the confidence and strength to show him kindness, even when it was hard. Oh, I still imagined I was throat punching him as I walked away from more of his harsh words. But I still walked away. Sure, I thought of reporting him, but something stopped me. There was something inside me that knew my grandmother's advice was right for the situation. Not that you shouldn't report someone if they are harassing you or hurting you, please know you have a right to do that.

One day, Sam shut my locker door as I was trying to get my books, and he mentioned something degrading about me going to a church youth group. I headed for the principal's office then changed my mind. Something had to be making him so mean.

For the next two years, I showed him kindness. A good morning. A smile. An offer of a piece of gum. Sharing notes if he was absent so he didn't fall behind… and he was absent a lot.

Then, before we graduated, he came up to me and asked how come I'd been so nice to him when he was so mean to me.

I replied: "Because I chose, and I will continue to choose, kindness." Those few words softened his face. His posture folded like a cheap suit. A smile broke out across his face.

I knew that the valuable lesson my grandma taught me had paid off. Finally, after all those years of being nice to Sam, I got to experience the life changing experience that kindness offers. From that day forward Sam and I were friends.

We became close friends after that. He shared the struggles he had been going through in his home. And then we both went off to college in different states and kept in touch with the occasional phone call and old-fashioned letters.

He told me in a heartfelt letter that he felt I possessed something intrinsic that he wanted. Joy and peace.

He sent me videos from his travels to the rainforests and from retreats all over the world where he learned about calmness and nature and woodworking. I will never forget one video from Thailand where he was in front of a giant golden statue, and he was glowing even more, a goofy thumbs up and mouthing, "I get it now."

Five years later, he returned home. His parents had passed. We began dating, then married, and took over the small farm his parents had. He invited artists to stay and practice their craft. He began designing and building magnificent pieces of furniture from trees that had felled naturally, or rescued old trees like yours, Aurora. He made Freedom's cradle before we even conceived her. His vision was and is so clear.

He became someone who makes everyone feel like a somebody.

I know my kindness helped make that happen. And the kindness of others. And the kindness within him that had been locked away.

We all have that power, Aurora.

You and Stella are discovering it on this wonderful quest of yours.

Here, I have a gift for you. It's a journal and inside is a little mirror you can see yourself in. Look at your beautiful soul through this mirror on the inside cover and then write your story, your wishes, your kindness, your words.

Now let's go and watch a negotiation of love and peace.

By the way, you look beautiful in that shade of green.

You can believe it and answer thank you. You don't have to think of a put down. Yes, I saw your mouth ready to dismiss the compliment.

Positive self-talk, Aurora. Check.

Nothing magic about that… Stella told me about the Questlisting.

8. QUESTLIST FINDINGS AND THE STRAWBERRY FARM

Pretty nice of Owl to drop us across town, huh?

All we have to do is go down to thirtieth and catch the Silverthorn route, then walk about an hour and we'll be there. Thank you for doing this with me, Stella.

And great idea to use our student bus passes. You should consider a career in banking, you're so good at saving money.

It's easy to save when you don't have any, or much, money to spend. You have no choice but to make something from nothing.

Run, there's the bus. Let's try to catch it.

Maybe he'll have to stop at the lights. He is stopping at the lights. Run faster.

I can't remember being this out of breath. I didn't do track like you did.

This body is in pretty good shape still. It might not look perfect to some, but it's perfect for me. Positive self-talk. Check. Positive body image. Check.

I've wanted to go out past Silverthorn for a long time. We need to get off at the last stop. When he reaches the turnaround and starts the route back.

The concession being closed while they pop in new water lines and haul out the tree means we don't miss a shift.

I need to erase the movie in my head of Tree being cut down.

Nova

You didn't have to watch.

Of course I had to watch.

You're brave, Aurora.

You're a true friend, Stella.

What if you picture the victory instead? Remember the cheers? I mean that great big wrestler guy lifted you on his shoulders. Like, how did that feel? The council accepted Sam and Magdalena's proposal.

And you made that happen, Stella. You went and found them. I was chained to the tree.

You did it all.

We did it all. You, me, Pinky, Owl, Sam, Magdalena, the wrestler guy, all the people, and even the city council.

When the wood from Tree is dried, Sam is going to call and I'm going to help build the benches for the rest of the summer. They say I can stay at their farm. Stella, will your grandpa be upset I'm not going to stay with you guys?

He'll be cool.

What about you? Will you be upset I'm not gonna stay with you?

Hey, you're not moving to the other side of the world. Friendship doesn't end when we're not together, besides that's two weeks from now. I'm on my own journey too, you know. It's weird but when I was tracking down Sam and Magdalena, I felt something. Like I was valuable to you. And to the world. I didn't understand it. Still don't. It's a weird feeling. You know what I mean?

Worthiness. I'm figuring that out too.

Worthy-ness. Like having a valued role.

Nova

Did you tell your grandpa you're going to not be in the campground park for a couple of nights?

What do you think?

Stella, you promised to tell him where we were going. If something happens us...

Nothing will happen to us.

That's what people say right before things happen to them.

You know what was great? Seeing your face on the news' websites... Sam showed me on his phone. We still haven't charged ours by the way. It's like we've not even been needing the phones. You know when professors go away from teaching for a while? Sabbaticals? Well, I feel we've been on an electronic sabbatical. The journey to the mountain to meditate, except we don't meditate. And there aren't any caves.

Sam showed me those images too. You weren't on any of them. You should have been.

I was busy.

This is the last stop. We've got about an hour's walk to get to the old barn and the closed-down strawberry farm one of my foster parents told me my mom used to work at. Make sure you say thank you to the bus driver. I'm pretty sure he knows we're not in summer school.

Thank you, sir. We have some freshly baked banana bread from Pinky, our erm, teacher. We hope you enjoy it.

And we can catch this bus back into the city from here, right? In a couple of days?

How far do we have to walk? Is this the wrong road?

I don't remember it like this. There's a whole new

neighborhood here. There was only a little chapel, like a bit bigger than a shed, but not all these houses.

Well, they do look new. Wait here. Just wait. I have an idea.

You just went right up to those landscaping ladies and talked to them.

They're not aliens.

I wish I wasn't as shy as I am.

But you have a good sense of direction. They both said the same thing. We're on the right road. That little church is about a mile down this road which will end as a paved road and turn into a dirt road and then farmland. Then the strawberry farm is another three miles farther.

You were ages with them. What else did they say? You didn't invite them over, did you? To the strawberry farm.

Do you think I'm some kind of idiot? I didn't even mention the strawberry farm. They did. I said we were meeting our hiking group west of the church, but we thought we were lost. Anyway, once they bought that lie, they told me they're starting a bit of a community drop-in for city kids to meet farming kids. No one's using the old church, apparently. And they said... when we get there to stop and say hi to their mom, who is apparently a pastor in the city and has taken on this project. One of the landscapers even phoned her and said we were on our way.

They could be axe murderers or kidnappers or—

Or really nice people who are making an effort to bring communities together. Another Pinky and Owl. Think on that, Aurora, while I take some quiet time to think about church.

You, think about church? You, quiet time? Hey, Stella, talk to me.

Ohm.... Ohm...

Nova

There it is. Wow, they've painted it white and blue.

Hello, Pastor Jamieson. Hi!

They'll hear us.

That's the point. We've got faith as a category on our Questlist. Now we've got an expert—the pastor.

We don't know she's an expert.

She's a pastor! She's an expert in what she believes. And what she believes is her job. We don't have to believe what she believes. It's R&D.

Are and Dee?

Zonda the cosmetic YouTuber talks about it all the time. Research and development. We can ask Pastor Jamieson about faith then file it away as part of our Questlist findings.

We have Questlist findings? You have Questlist findings? Where is this file?

C'mon, Aurora. Get with it. Find that courage you had when you chained yourself to the tree. Stop being scared of people. Think of them as trees.

THE PASTOR SPEAKS

The girls called and said you would stop in. So glad you did. We're so proud of our daughters—best in the business. Doing plenty of work in Silverthorn. Good sense of adventure, like the two of you. And do they get teased by the men in the industry? Well, they used to, but they've shown what they're made of. Confidence and goodness. Of course, like a lot of parents, I hoped at least one of them would follow in my footsteps, to the church, but in a way they have. They may not have a church and a congregation—mine is over in Riverview—but they show kindness to others, they're honest, and they help others whenever they can. Church isn't just for Sundays. And it's not just a building, either. Like this old church here. The kids will come in. They will create a feeling of fellowship whenever they're here.

Nova

Now, when you sat down, and we poured you some sun-brewed iced tea, you asked a powerful question, Stella, that I wish more people would ask. "What is faith?" And then your friend apologized for the ask. Aurora, there's never any reason to apologize for asking. And this is a big ask. And I love big asks. God loves big asks. The God of my understanding does anyway.

Sure, your question could have been as simple as the one you asked my daughters. You know, like asking for directions to a destination. But in a way, maybe that's what faith is too. It's a direction. And it's a destination.

Sometime, when it's quiet in your mind, try stripping away all the things you are: student, friend, customer, bus passenger, hiker. Take away all the roles until you have removed everything and there is only one thing left. That thing is your essence, the spark that is you, the energy, some would call it your soul. I call it the soul. When you can feel that inside, then you are well on your way to discovering the meaning of life, the meaning of faith, the meaning of everything.

Don't force any understanding and, by all means, keep asking questions, and trust that there is something larger than all of us. Listen to the stories of others, all the stories. Sort them out and decide what you resonate with. Listen to the homeless person on the street, and the woman from the agency who comes to check on the woman on the street, listen to recordings or read the works of the giants of change: Martin Luther King, Mother Teresa, Nelson Mandela, Albert Schweitzer, Bishop Desmond Tutu, Jesus, the authors of the Gospels, the great poets and philosophers: Thoreau, Whitman, Emerson. And listen to little children too.

Each person has their own take on faith, even those within the same religion or community.

The God of your understanding is whatever you decide it means or stands for. It's a source of creation or power greater than you and yet still a part of you. You don't have to be affiliated with a certain group or church to be full of faith.

I am a Christian. I believe in God, and Jesus Christ being the son of God. I believe I was created by God, in his image. I believe God created man and woman with divine equality and worth.

I believe the grace that God offers is wildly undeserved—meaning God is so forgiving and many of us do a lot of things that require forgiveness. I was raised a Christian, but it wasn't until I was in my twenties that I decided not to attend church anymore. I wanted to figure out my faith on my own. I decided it was time to study and choose my faith based upon my studies, research, and reflection; not what someone preached to me while growing up.

During that time, I abandoned my mindset and the formal teachings about religions that I'd been taught, told, or influenced to believe—those that included hypocrisy, judgment, and shame. I began to understand, for the first time, that the God of the Bible I was taught from was in fact not at all judgmental, he was full of love. He did not want us to feel shame, nor for us to shame others. He accepted all people. From all faiths and with all faiths. Even without faith.

I believe Jesus touched the sick, communed with the broken, and defended the weak. Those are exactly the people that many in my church would shame. I learned to not put my faith in the people that were casting stones as they walked the halls of the church, but to put my faith in God.

My faith grew stronger than ever.

I mean, let's face it: we are all broken, we are all weak at times, and that's why I lean so much on my faith. My faith has taught me to love all people. All people.

The theologies—the rules—of the church I was raised in were built upon a fragile system. I believe our purpose on earth is to love and be a reflection of God and to care for the widows and orphans and to speak up for those who cannot speak for themselves. That's part of why I am so passionate about children. That is why I want to start this community, out here where the big city and the country folk are neighbors.

My faith has become the foundation of who I am. What I mean by that is I have found the belief system inside me that allows me to recognize all belief systems are valuable if they are based on loving others, supporting each other, recognizing we are each other's brothers and sisters.

It is important to me, and it's always a part of me, whether it's at home eating dinner with the girls or helping them with a job they can't quite finish on time or when I am giving a sermon—which is really just a conversation—in my church in Riverview. I am not an in-your-face Christian. I think I'm a smile-at-your-face helper.

This little building here, where so many worshipped in the past, has a lovely energy, and I don't intend to turn it into a place where I'm all preachy. Yet I shall reach into my faith to put a foundation of kindness into this building. In the tables and chairs we put in, the games we stock on the shelves, the flowers we plant, the community garden we will introduce, and the after-school exchanges.

I hope that makes sense. If not now, then maybe later. There's no time limit on growth and understanding, and there are no rules as to how a person travels their faith journey. Helping others is prayer, so is being alone and imagining goodness for the less fortunate. Asking for something for yourself isn't selfish either. The conversations you have with God are your private business. Between God and you. Even the name you call God may be different. We don't all speak the same language on earth… not with our voices. But we can with our intentions.

Now, I've probably exhausted you. I know you want to walk to whatever it is you're doing with this hiking club. So, feel free to use the washroom, hang around or even grab a paintbrush—if not today, then another day. Who knows, maybe we'll cross paths again. I've got another daughter and grandbaby way down this highway and south a bit. The world is a small place in an endless sea of love. Life is a small part of an eternal journey.

Aurora, I think we've walked a hundred miles.

We've been walking for about half an hour. I can see ahead where the road divides. I remember it. We're almost there.

And that whole hundred miles is just wearing me out—

Half hour, tops.

Okay, okay, so not a hundred miles. But this whole time I've been thinking about what she said.

Those kinds of thoughts can make half an hour seem like a hundred miles, huh?

Deep?

Deep.

Were you thinking about what she said?

I'm still thinking about what she said.

But guess what?

Don't think it's possible to guess with you anymore.

Questlisting. Faith. Check. Got me some information for my foundation.

Nova

You can say that again. No... don't.

I love the tent Owl loaned us, but I still want to sleep outside. Now we just have to wait for the stars. Think how many more we're gonna see without the glow of the city.

We're not that far from it. The bus stop is an hour from here. I can see the skyline of the southern part of downtown.

Hey, it's far enough away. I'm going for a walk to see if there are any rogue strawberries. Coming?

I got something else to do.

Come with me. There's strawberries in them hills.

I'll go tomorrow. You go. Unless you're scared of nature. You scared of the forest?

I'm not afraid of anything.

Mirror, mirror… I have too many freckles.

No you don't. Negative self-talk.

I thought you were gone, Stella. I do have a lot of freckles.

Then who were you talking to? Ah, the book with a mirror behind the cover? Is that from Maggie? Sheesh, all I have is a spoon.

An IHOP spoon by any chance?

Do your thing with the mirror book. And when you look at yourself don't put yourself down. That's what's not attractive. Catch this pen. Write a bestseller. I'm going to find some strawberries.

Nova

AURORA'S JOURNAL ENTRY

Dear book with a mirror, made by Magdalena, that is now my book that I wish will one day be the world's book. Right now, I'm making notes while I still discover. This is a work in progress. So am I.

My book to change the world, or a tiny corner of it.
Ways to make everybody feel like somebody:

- Smile at everyone you meet.
- Be kind. It costs nothing and can mean everything to someone else.
- Thank people for serving you even if you are paying them for it.
- Treat everyone the same—we all have the same human value.
- Stand up for others.

Gratitude. Check. Kindness. Check.

AURORA MEETS BERNICE

Hi. Oh, I didn't mean to scare you. There's usually no one out here. I'm Bernice. Bernie for short. Oh, no, I've interrupted your journaling.

I'm sorry. We didn't think we were doing any harm. Is this your land?

No. It's okay, you're not trespassing. I'm just acquainted with this area. I've been coming to walk here a couple of times a week for years. I work shifts at the Misericordia hospital at the city's limits, so when I'm on nights, I come here in the day. I've never slept out here though. You're going to do that? Alone?

I'm with a friend. She'll be back any moment.

Oh, I didn't mean to scare you. Look there's my car and I'll go back to it. But it's clever to say you're not alone.

You didn't scare me. Well, maybe a little bit. But I really am out here with a friend.

It's a comfy seat huh? I love that old plank propped up with some tires.

Did you make it?

You're intuitive. I like to sit out here and think. That's what you're doing isn't it?

Something like that.

Why this spot?

Erm... no reason.

It's okay, you don't have to tell me. This place has a lot of history. Lots of people have worked here over the years. When I was a kid, my sister and I worked picking berries out here. A bunch of us would hop into the back of the farmer's pickup and get a couple of bucks a basket. The barn looked a bit different then. The ground too. I even know what truck those tires are from.

Do you want some water?

I've got some in my pack thanks, but I'll sit for a bit if you don't mind. And I'll hydrate. Here, have an energy bar.

What do you do at the hospital?

I'm a nurse. I love it. I've worked in the neonatal unit for a while. Babies who need extra help.

Sweet.

What do you do?

I'm... Aurora. I mean, I'm a student. And I've got a part time job at the campground in the city, and in a couple of weeks I'm going to help build benches at a farm about a half hour's drive from here.

You sound surprised, like no one's ever asked you. Oh. Let me guess. No one's ever asked you.

Bernie, I've never even asked myself.

You're going to be out at Sam and Magdalena's place? The HeART Center?

How did you know?

They're all that is down that way, and you've got one of her handmade journals. I have one too.

Does yours have a mirror?

All Maggie's journals do. She's all about the inner journey and looking into your own soul. Have you done that?

I'm literally on the first page.

I've filled a few of her books, and more notebooks before that. It's good to see someone as young as you using it. You'll be safe that way. Safe through strength. Strength through understanding the self.

Safe through strength?

People who do not discover their worth can get caught up in some scary situations. Somehow I can tell you're not into drugs or alcohol. But for those who are, it's such a tough road to come back from. Some do not. My sister did not.

I'm sorry, Bernie.

People need a whole lotta courage to say no; they need to know themselves and be aware and still that might not be enough if they're predisposed to addiction.

Mega strength and some kind of luck?

Aurora, some people are not like you. They are not sensitive to people and places and situations. Some people can see injuries, like a broken leg, and get that someone hit a bump in the road and fell off their bike. They can see a cut from a sharp vegetable knife and know that the person needs stitches. And they can feel badly for a person who has tested positive for a disease like cancer. But, when it comes to being empathetic to those who have mental health issues, addiction issues, depression, and chemical imbalances, they can't see the injury or illness in the same way. And when people can't see it the same way, they judge, and those who are addicted are not seen or heard the way others are. And even when they are seen, those victims are so vulnerable. I'm sorry… this is a place where I ramble. I'd usually be talking to the dirt, and that hill over there.

I had to come here. This is going to sound crazy: I knew but didn't know someone who was addicted.

Me too. That's why I come.

Nova

THE STORY OF BERNIE'S SISTER

Aurora, do you mind if I stay a while and tell you a story?

My best friend and I were two years apart. We spent much of our childhood exploring the woods, digging for crawdads in the creek, challenging each other in sports until after dark almost every night. We fished together, watched our favorite college basketball team together, and got into mischief together. She drove me crazy, we fought, made up and fought again.

My best friend was my sister. I looked up to her. Atlas was a talented athlete. Competitive and a straight A student; several schools offered her scholarships. Everyone always thought things came easy to Atlas. No one knew that behind closed doors, when she looked into the mirror, she saw a different person than we saw.

As her senior year rolled around, she planned to accept a scholarship from Columbia University. She was going to study medicine and become a surgeon.

But during that year, some of her friends started experimenting with drugs. Atlas did too.

Soon Atlas was using drugs to numb the pain of everyday life, even though it wasn't obvious that someone as clever and athletic and friendly as Atlas had everyday life problems. People thought she had it made.

Before I knew it, before my parents knew it, Atlas's life spiraled out of control, and fast. The drugs were in charge.

Those bright and promising plans of Atlas's didn't ever materialize. Instead of spending the next eighteen years watching my sister excel as a woman, our family spent eighteen years praying and worrying. We spent eighteen years wondering if we'd ever get our Atlas back. Eighteen years receiving calls from authorities, hospitals, and people from her inner circle letting us know her drug use landed her in jail, in the hospital, and even in the ditch. The substances that robbed my sister of her fulfilling her life were also the substances that took away my parents' peace. Atlas's substance abuse didn't just ruin Atlas's life, it affected our entire family.

Imagine being a prisoner to a substance. Imagine doing whatever you can to come up with the money to pay for the substances that your body is so addicted to, even going so far as stealing from your own family. Imagine disappointing your closest friends and family. Imagine sitting in jail because the stealing caught up to you and you've no one left willing to bail you out one more time. Imagine sleeping on the floor of a cold, filthy park bathroom because you have nowhere to live. Now, imagine your family reaching a point where they know if they don't do something you'll end up dead, so they take the heartbreaking step of granting the state guardianship, which is when you lose the right to make any decisions about your own life. Imagine living in a group home, even though you're a grown-up, with people you don't want to live with. If you can imagine all of that, you're imagining a life in the grips of the demons we call substances.

Drugs and other substances took my sister's potential from us all. They took the things my sister was capable of and supposed to accomplish, all the years I was supposed to enjoy encouraging and praising and following her example as she pursued the things that set her soul on fire. Drugs robbed her of a fulfilling future. Notice I didn't say "borrowed." I said "took." Those things were gone. Gone forever. Gone. Forever. The last place I saw her was here.

Most people who become addicted first start using drugs and alcohol believing they won't lose control, that the substances won't have a negative impact on their lives. They think they'll try this drug or have that one drink, just once. It'll be fun. Harmless.

But sometimes the drugs aren't even the drugs the person thinks they're getting. Stuff is added to those illicit drugs they think are harmless. Poisons. The people who are getting rich off them are either cutting them with something so they can make more money from the same amount of the core drug, or they're cutting them with something that's going to make people keep coming back for more. It may sound evil, but it is simple economics.

The second danger is that drugs and alcohol are so effective at blunting the impact of our emotions that the artificial high doesn't feel so artificial. And the real world begins to look pretty sad. The body and mind demand more drugs to keep the façade of happiness.

Atlas's future was created by the substances she thought would numb the pain she was trying to mask. This glimpse into her story isn't even a fraction of the sadness, loneliness, gut-wrenching life her addiction has dealt her. At some point a person has to find the strength to deal with this kind of loss. My family, I, never knew where she was or is, if she settled down and was too scared to come back into our lives, or if she…

Someone in her old gang told me the last time they saw her she was pregnant. They were going to meet me, here, and bring her. They never showed.

The End. I mean The End.

Nova

Bernice, I'm so sorry.

I'm sorry, Aurora. I don't mean to overwhelm you. But I can't not share what I know. So, if ever you feel like you're not handling your emotions well, ask someone who you know is not involved in drugs, for advice. There are even help lines you can call. I volunteer at one.

I didn't mean to bring you down on your own retreat here. It really was a beautiful place. So full of life. So filled with dreams. And the strawberries were a color I've never matched before, except, except maybe your hair, that's it, when the sun touches your hair, it reminds me of those strawberries. And Atlas. She had hair just like yours.

I'm sorry, again. I've made you cry. You know what I'm talking about don't you? But it's not you who is the addict. You'll never take drugs, will you? You know someone who did.

The problem is I know but don't know someone who did.

Someone like Atlas?

Bernice, did you know Atlas is another word for map? I just wrote her name in my journal and realized that.

She's in your journal?

She's in my mirror.

I don't understand. And I need to get back to my car and head to work. Will you be here tomorrow? Can I bring you and your friend something? Pay you back for listening to me.

You already did.

Will you be okay? Will your friend be back soon? I can check on you after my shift.

It's okay. I am on a quest. And now I have a map. Go take care of the babies, Bernice.

Oh, Aurora, that hair. Strawberries.

Nova

STELLA RETURNS

Strawberries! Tiny dried-up strawberries. Imagine they do not look like pimples.

Stella, you are disgusting. How many did you find?

Whose water container?

She'll come back for it tomorrow. I don't want to be here when she does, okay?

She? Was she a bully? Did she hurt you? I shouldn't have left.

She's a nurse. She's a guide. She is nice. I need to decide on my terms when I want to see her.

When? Why didn't you say "if" you want to see her? It's not like you have to. Do you know where she lives or something?

I know where she works.

There's more isn't there?

I have to work it out first.

Here, have one of these. Pretend they're strawberry flavored candy Lifesavers.

9. STORIES IN THE STARS

You're driving me insane, Aurora. First, we had to come out here. Now, you want to leave before that Bernie nurse you met today comes back tomorrow?

Stel, I'm not saying we go back today. Can we just enjoy being under the stars out here and then in the morning pack up and leave? Can we do that without any questions?

So you might want to see this woman again, but not tomorrow. And it has something to do with this old strawberry farm, the color of your hair, and addiction? Did she offer you something?

Not what you're thinking. And I don't even think she realized she was opening a bit of a messy box of memories I have but don't have.

Eat some banana bread. Let's stare at the stars. I'm ready for one of your stories.

Can you keep a secret?

I am a vault.

If you are, it's only because you have no access to social media. Wait, I didn't mean it that way. That was mean. I was going to say I was joking, and I was, but I do trust you. I just don't always trust myself. Look, I don't want to announce this to the world, but I need to share it with someone so that I can believe in it. And, in a way, I want to share it with one person but not ever have that person say, "I thought you were going to do that thing, and you haven't." I don't need another "me" in my head.

I have no idea what you are saying. You want to tell one person something. That one person is me. You don't want me to know?

I want to tell one person. I want that person to be you. Once I've told you, I don't want you to say, like, in two weeks or six months, "Hey, that thing you told me about? Where is it? I thought you were making something?" Like no pressure. Accountability and support but not pressure. Do you know what I mean?

You are one complicated strawberry, Aurora.

I'm gonna tell you the secret.

I'm gonna keep your secret.

I'm writing a book.

You're the perfect person for writing a book. I mean how perfect is this that you write a book. You've read so many. Is it for little kids? Is it another version of Anne of Green Gables? Who is the main character? Hey! Am I in it? Can you name a character after me?

Stell-ll-ll-ah!

There's no one else here. I'm not blowing your secret. I'm interested. I'm asking. When you decided you'd write a book, how did you decide?

That's the thing. I didn't. It decided. It chose me.

Okay, that's a bit spooky.

It's real. It's been "hosting" us the whole time. It's there, out there, not on a bookshelf in a store, or at the click of a buy-now, but out there as in, well, out there, in its own constellation, all we have to do is reach for it.

Okay, now you've gone too far. That's just too freaky.

I knew I shouldn't have told you.

No, no. You should have. You did. It's okay. I scare easily when it comes to things I can't see. You said we.

All of us. The collective of girls, Stella. That group of children who were told that when they grew up, they'd change the world. We're no longer those children but we don't know if we're at that point where we are changing the world. We're like the lost boys in *Peter Pan*, except we're the lost girls, or the forgotten girls.

Let's face it, Aurora, when it comes to being not children and not adults, all boys and girls are in the same category.

See, you are good at pointing things out. That's why this is a "we." We're all writing in our own ways. Living our stories. Happy endings, tragic endings, city stories, country stories, stand on top of the mountain and shout "I am alive" stories.

People choose to do stuff, Aurora. Not the other way around. Besides, if it's already out there, let someone else get it off the ethereal—ya know like a kind of otherworldly ghostly shelf—and pass it around. I'm asking you to ease up, if you didn't choose to, then don't do it.

I have to. I've been called. There are things I don't understand that are jumping out at me.

You're hallucinating.

We both ate the same banana bread, Stel. This is real. Not some fantasy. I've done more so far this week than I've ever done in my life… step out into a quest.

That last part, yeah. It's the same for me. I've never been without a phone. I'd never slept under the stars. I'd never returned anything I'd stolen… and I did, Aurora, I returned that fork.

All the things others have shared, stuff from your grandpa, stuff from Miss Frankie, Pinky, Owl, Magdalena, Sam, even the creators of those original stories that I retold… then those landscapers you went to—women who were totally rocking it—and their mom, a pastor, and what she told us… it keeps shooting into my mind and I don't understand it all.

You will, Aurora. You will. That's something that just shot into my mind. Hey, universe! Stop with your powerful shooting arrows into the mind. I'm not ready. It's freaking me out.

Nova

The more you focus on what you don't want, the more you'll get what you don't want. Trust me, I've been asking the universe to stop shooting those mind arrows, those idea arrows, for days and it's just sending more. It's like some teacher in detention doubling the time when you screw around.

Ouch. Enough. Send that message to Aurora not me you stupid, sharp stick.

More arrows?

Massive ones.

Maybe I'm focusing on getting arrows, and so it's sending more. So what if I focus on, say, helping you with the book, will stuff come at me that will help me help you write the book?

You're dizzying me more than the arrows. Do you mean like if I focus on cramps from my period that I will pay more attention to them so it will seem like there are more, but if I focus on the fact there's no pain in my hand or foot that I won't notice the cramps as much?

Maybe it's not the focus, but the actual rhythm of healing that comes from positive focus at other times, or all the time. Like any particular moment or day, focus on say, the feet and how great they are. Not just remembering them when an ankle is sprained, but in the way of, "Hey, feet, thank you for carrying me around all the time." It's kind of a like a daily gratitude for my body is working as nature intended. Oh no, where did those gems come from? The arrows meant for you are landing in my head.

Like there is a power greater than us. There is a source we can plug into. Everything we do and say matters to our growth. Not just surviving but thriving. Through being thankful. For life.

It's God.

Maybe it is. I don't know. It's bigger in that when we're doing all that surviving or thriving, we're teaching others how to treat us. Barely survive and be negative, roll over and don't stand up for ourselves, and the kind of people that come into our lives will be perfect for treating us as if we don't matter. Thrive and be confident and positive and the kind of people that show up will treat us with respect.

Don't say anything. I want to think about that. Focus. Power. You're writing a book. Vision. Oh-my-freaky-grandma's-big-toe ... a book. Your book. I see it.

Okay, I am thinking of the book I'm writing. I see it. It's not so imaginary. It's there.

I see it too. It's beautiful. Your name on the front cover and all.

Reach into the stars. Open a page from the book you see up there. What does it say?

I opened it at chapter seven. The title is bolded. It says, "The Courage to Sit at Any Table." What the heck does that mean?

I don't know yet. But if we start at chapter one, I bet we will. Can you close it now and see that your name is on the front too?

I'm too busy with the any table thing. I've got all kinds of tables in my head. How am I going to sleep? There's one with white linen and fancy silverware. The wooden chair frame in front of me is like stiff white lace; I'm afraid to pull it out, let alone sit on it.

But you are meant to sit there. Look at the place card. A piece of folded paper near the plate.

How did you know? It has my name on it. In calligraphy.

Can you see the ornately forged spoon beside it?

Very funny. What about my bedtime story?

Stella, you are your story.

I want one from you.

Nova

Look in the spoon. You need the one in the spoon.

Hello spoon.

Questlisting. Confidence. Check. Positive self-talk. Check. Positive body image. Check. I still gotta figure that one out. I mean I walked a hundred miles today. I feel a bit stiff, so I know I'm taking care of my body, but I feel like I'm missing something. I'm putting it on a "discuss with Aurora" note. Gratitude. Check. Pinky, props to you, you make amazing banana bread. Pastor Jamieson, you gave me a lifetime of Sunday school in one afternoon. Kindness. Check. I want to help others. I'm excited to get back to help Pinky and Owl, not just for my paycheck. And I want to take my grandpa to a film festival of old westerns. Starting to understand faith. Check.

Stella, are you finished? I can hear you. Why are you such a night owl?

I'm speaking aloud because I'm practicing my voice.

Can you do it without speaking? I know, don't

answer. I was joking.

Aurora, what is positive body image?

It's the opposite of negative body image.

Aurora, what is negative body image? Do not say the opposite of a positive body image.

Can't you just ask something simpler—like how many stars are in the sky?

Aurora, pleeeease.

You're not giving up this Questlist are you? You're really serious about it all.

You know you are too. Self-image... body image... I know it's more than wanting bigger boobs, bigger butts, and fewer zits.

It's something about how the wanting happens, and how strong the wanting is. It's... it's... wait, it's about the feelings that come along and smack you in the face when you're in front of the mirror and you're disappointed with what you see, and all the things you learned in kindergarten about "free to be me," "I'm special," and "everybody belongs" just disappear and are replaced by... erm...

Insults?

That and statements. Like everybody belongs except every body doesn't belong. Your body doesn't belong. Not yours, but that's the statement that would come from the me in the mirror.

And questions. How could you even wear shorts when your knees look like that? Not yours, mine.

And comparisons. Like the me in the mirror has a voice that just comes out in my own head and says, look at your cheeks, they're like a chipmunk's. Then that message stays with me all day, when I'm around others, then I am comparing myself to others and seeing how big my cheeks are. Then I don't even need the mirror because that evil mirror has moved inside my head.

You know what's weird about that? You love chipmunks. Remember when we hiked with the class and there were those little guys—but I'm not saying your cheeks are like chipmunks' but if they were, you love all those squirrely creatures. They're so cute.

Are you saying that we might love things in others but not ourselves? Like we are never satisfied?

What the heck happens after kindergarten to make us not like ourselves? Is there some kind of black hole we go into over the summer holidays where we come back at six or seven years old on diets and comparing our looks to others?

Well, let's say you had an older sister or a mom…

We don't have mothers.

But let's say there are influences where we grow up that are totally not satisfied with the way they look.

Nova

Then we'd pick that up, right?

I'm glad it's dark so I don't see your eyes rolling, but Aurora, Zonda talks about this on her videos. She does go a bit all, "Let's do this celebrity and that celebrity look." She has those specials, but she always says at the end, this is playtime, and that makeup is not to uncreate who we are but to have fun with who we are.

A regular sage, huh?

I mean it. She's not all over the "be like me" or "be like that celebrity." She's more the "be yourself and enjoy yourself." You gotta watch her.

So, what is it? What is a positive body image? Is it the same as a healthy body image?

Okay, Stella, I give, you crazy questlister. A positive body image is being comfortable with and accepting the way you look.

Then a negative body image is feeling unhappy with the way you look. Like really unhappy. Enough to want to change your body size—for the wrong reasons. To be a follower of others because you don't like yourself, you think you're not good enough—hello, self-confidence, they're linked.

Changing your body to be healthier, like being able to not be out of breath when you run up a flight of stairs, is a good thing. But changing it because you think you are nothing, a nobody, a loser, is not healthy. It's negative. And if that mirror is in your face all day, then that's a problem. Agreed?

I just realized something. Remember Elizabeth Castle in sixth grade?

She was really popular, and wore cool clothes, and then she started missing school. The teacher told us she'd moved.

That's her. Well, once, I saw her at the mall and hardly recognized her. She had lost so much weight.

Nova

Grandpa saw her parents at the hospital. He told me not to tell. So, I didn't. But I am now. He said she went to the hospital to fix her hate. I just thought he was mispronouncing some illness... you know how he is with his words... but I just realized he wasn't wrong. The mirror became a monster for her and started taking over her mind. She didn't see herself for real.

Extreme. Wow. I mean there's stuff I don't like about myself, but a mirror-mind zombie?

How does a person not cross that line?

Well, I don't hate everything about myself, but hearing about Elizabeth scares me. I think we have to get used to being positive about ourselves.

Like a gardener and a garden.

What does dirt have to do with makeup, fitting into skinny jeans, and wishing for no freckles?

It's the word cultivate. If a person can grow a

garden, with different veggies and fruits, then people can take care of themselves and grow a positive body image. Except for the gardener, weeding is important, and the rake is their friend. For the person who is growing themselves, then the mirror has to become the friend. Selfies have to become other-ies. I mean we could take pictures of ourselves, but not for the same reason, not for comparing. Cultivate a positive body image.

Stella, you're amazing. You saw yourself in the spoon and you made it a tool. Maggie knows it too. She puts mirrors in her journals. The words we speak to ourselves matter, and it's so powerful when we can see ourselves speaking them to ourselves.

Words start with thoughts. Thoughts that are negatives or positives that we think over and over and over are powerful.

Stella! Those thoughts thought over and over become our beliefs.

Is all this about self-image, self-talk, confidence, gratitude, kindness really all about faith?

Well, faith is a belief system.

It's all connected, Aurora. It's all connected. That university student was sure on to something, huh?

Stella, you took that list a lot further, and we narrowed it to a pretty amazing group of qualities that are, well…

Lifesaving.

For sure lifemaking.

Same thing.

10. AURORA AND HER BIRTHMOTHER

Stella, you were talking in your sleep.

Aurora, you were snoring.

Don't you want to know what you said?

We need to pack up. You wanted to leave before that Bernie woman comes.

You were rambling about family. Over and over, the word: family. First I thought you were saying Emily—remember that really friendly girl at school who put notes with happy messages on everyone's locker?

Every person has an energy, even those we read about, and they are all members of one family. We are all connected. We are never alone.

Whoa, Stel. Can I put that in the book? Can you say it again so I can write it? I wish our phones were charged so we could record this. Then it would be fast, and we could move on before nurse Bernie gets here.

Behind the shed, you did cover your pee with dirt, right?

Like a cat.

Okay, I'll say it while I pack and clean up our mess. You get it down in your journal.

Leave my bus pass on top. That's the first thing I'll need. Okay, I'm ready. Go.

Hello beautiful people, this is Stella, the female Aristotle, philosopher for today. Today's message is a request from Aurora of Lindsay Woods. Every person has an energy. We are one human family. The same sky is above us all. We wish on the same falling stars. We all have something to cry about. We all pee our pants laughing... well, most of us.

That's not what you said the first time.

It's an edit.

Try harder. Something about we all have energy.

Well, of course we do. We'd be dead if we didn't.

But would we? When we are dead where does the energy go?

Agghhh, Aurora. Stop it. The idea arrows are killing me.

So where does your energy go?

Every person has an energy, even those we read about, and they are all members of one family. We are all connected. We are never alone.

Bingo.

Let's go. It's an hour to the bus stop.

Hopefully Bernie doesn't drive by and see us.

Oh, pul-ease. Stop with the Bernie. She's family. We're all family.

WHISPER

That is exactly what I'm afraid of.

Did you say something?

I asked you if you had your bus pass.

Nova

Aurora, stop looking over your shoulder. Stop counting steps. You're being paranoid. If she drives by, we can say hi and carry on.

What if I can't control myself and get into her car?

I gotta meet this nurse. What kind of power does she have to make you do that? You sure she didn't have a syringe of something she stuck in you?

That. Is. Not. Funny.

I can't help you if you don't talk to me. I haven't seen you this freaked out since you opened that envelope from the social worker—you know it had some stuff about your birthmother. Ohhhhhhhh! Is there a connection? The strawberry farm, Bernice, your birthmother?

Stella, shut up. Pick up the pace.

WHISPER

We are all family.

11. STELLA FINDS A TALISMAN

Aurora, guess what? The clowns from site four are gone. Pinky says they were taking advantage of her hospitality. Putting toilet paper and soap in their backpacks. She let them do it for a bit but finally talked to them, then they cut down a sapling. Wet stuff doesn't burn. Smoke everywhere. Damaging nature is her limit. She was crying over the young tree being hacked to the ground. Owl asked them to leave. They're going to see if they can save it. She told me some stuff about her first husband. That's why I've been a while. She sat me down and talked to me about the counselling she went through before and after she left him.

Oh, poor Pinky. It's like what Miss Frankie told me about the way we teach people how to treat us.

She must have had a bad relationship and thought she could be treated a certain way. Now, she knows not to let people treat her or the property in certain ways. She stands up for what she believes in. And she believes in herself. Her own power.

Don't look at me that way. I didn't say a word about you writing a book. I am a vault. Pinky said sometimes we come across people in our lives who test how much they can get away with by treating us poorly. They can do it in subtle ways, like sneakily clever, and you keep thinking you're the one that's "wrong." Gaslighting she called it. She said sometimes you can walk away from a relationship once you understand their ways. But sometimes, like if there was someone else working at the concession on the same shift and they were, you know, pushing you around, making you feel badly about yourself, then you have to go deep inside then speak up for yourself. That's hard. But there are people to help you do that, and books too. Like your book might do that. At least raise awareness.

Sounds like Pinky should write a book.

She said that it's important to draw boundaries. That "no" is a complete sentence. And to do it all with an attitude of respect for others. To not go low yourself.

Why would I act with respect toward someone who is being a jerk?

Don't make me dig for answers to concepts that are delivered by arrows.

Be the target for good, Stella. Please. This book is ours.

Write this down because I am not repeating it. And I'm not waiting until the phones are recharged. You did plug them in on Pinky's patio, didn't you?

Pen is ready.

Didn't you? Aurora? Put down the pen. Did you plug in the phones to charge so we'd have camera and recorder? And I can stop using the spoon, and you can stop using the mirror in the journal, and...

You have to use the spoon. I was meant to use the mirror in the journal. Don't you see? That's what we're supposed to do. When the phone's implanted in my hand, I can't hold the stars.

You said you'd charge the batteries.

I never held the stars before, Stella. I'm scared they'll disappear when I get my phone back.

You lied.

You'll stop getting idea arrows when you get yours back.

You deceived me.

I was going to tell you. At work tonight. In the concession.

Stop. Pick up your pen. I'm saying this once then I'm going for a walk. It's important to draw boundaries. That "no" is a complete sentence. And to do it all with an attitude of respect for others. To not go low yourself.

Nova

I was going to tell you in the concession because you wouldn't be able to walk away from there. You'd have to stay and talk about it.

I know you heard that.

Okay, now here's your phone. Pinky saw the cord wasn't in the outlet and did it for us. If you can catch it, then you can work out a way to balance the phone with the stars. If you miss, then your phone will be broken, and the decision made for you. I know I'm going to keep using spoon. And I'm going to get my phone plan back too.

Don't do that with my phone. Don't throw it. Stella... don't... aghhh

Whoa, Aurora, you should play some kind of ball sport. You caught that like your life depended on it.

When did you get so philosophical? When did you become this sage? Something's changed in you.

It's the magic spoon. Or the fact I spent the afternoon with Owl, playing Go Fish.

Seriously, the spoon is not magic. And Go Fish is not chess.

Think what you want. It's a free country. Your behavior is a reflection on you and your state of mind. A controlling person's behavior is a reflection of their state of mind. Don't lower yourself into the mud and fight with someone who is being disrespectful. Instead, do what they do not expect... like your Miss Frankie said, Owl had a similar story. He says show them respect. That will speak louder to them. This doesn't mean you have to be a doormat; it simply means you set boundaries. Take the high road.

And by the way, the spoon is fricking magic. I shall not be using my phone in place of the spoon. I will be using my phone to record my feelings.

Showing respect. Owl is wise. Oh, that's weird. But it makes sense, like Pinky did when she talked to those campers about the toilet paper and soap, still let them stay, but on their third strike they were out.

Hey, maybe that's how he got that name. If you don't want to know what he said, then you won't know if it's important for your book which, by the way, I've told no one about.

Okay, let's turn on the recorder on my phone. Tell me what he said. But first... can you forgive me?

Why? What have you done that I don't know about?

It's what you do know about. The phones.

Aurora, you are losing your edge. Or I am growing? I forgave you instantly. You probably need to forgive yourself.

Tell me what he said and help me grow. The phone's still recording.

I wrote it on the back of a camping invoice. The guy's a fricking self-help guide.

Don't become an approval addict.

Tune into your own needs.

Watch your self-talk.

Don't speak badly about yourself.

Don't let your mistakes or weaknesses define you.

Remind yourself of your strengths and qualities.

Being different is a blessing, not a curse.

Respecting yourself is loving who you are, wholly.

Don't let anybody force you to be or do anything you don't want to be or do

Don't violate your own morals and convictions.

Learn as much as possible.

Be responsible and do the things you need to do.

Lean on a faith, your own faith.

That's a lot to unpack, Stel.

Why do you think I wrote it down? Owl has a faith. A faith in an all-loving energy he chooses, like many, to call God. There are other names for God. He has a set of golden rules he follows that align with his beliefs that he formed in what he calls his terrible twenties. He didn't elaborate. I didn't ask. There weren't that many invoices to write on.

Stella, you are the best researcher. And we have to make sure Pinky and Owl are in our acknowledgements in the book.

We need more than my research. And a set of easy-to-remember points.

Okay, go. How do you make self-respect a top priority?

Surround yourself with positive people.

You're saying quality not quantity.

Four true friends or even one is better than a hundred that have sketchy attitudes. Your turn, Aurora.

Don't settle for less.

Less than what?

Hmmm. Less than… less than you deserve.

What about when people think they deserve nothing?

This is deep.

Words are cheap. We have to say what "don't settle for less" means. If we don't know then how will the reader know?

Let's change it to: "get to know yourself, discover your value to the world, and then never let that go. Stay true to your discovery of worthiness. Never let anyone take that away from you."

Well, it's longer, but it gets the job done. You were typing between our conversation. Read me the list of what you've been putting down.

Forgive yourself

Forgive others

Be confident

Be honest

Honor your body

Nourish your mind

Stop comparing

It helps if you've got someone to model yourself after.

This is flagged for more work. I never had many teachers.

Just because your mom isn't around and mine is dead doesn't mean we don't have examples. Miss Frankie, Pinky, Owl, Magdalena, Sam... remember we're all one family.

Stella, I just think the arrows that have been hitting you struck me. How's this: there will always be someone who *cannot* see your worth. Don't let it be you!

You know, Aurora, it's all fine when we're not in a large group. We're hanging with wise elders, in nature, and with each other. Once we're back at school, in September, and I know you will, I'm not sure about me, then we'll be with others. It won't be so easy to be, what do you call it? Reflective. Self-reflective.

So, we'll need some tools. Not just our thoughts.

Like screwdrivers and saws?

Like props in a play. But on the stage of ourselves. A bracelet that jingles. An alarm on the phone. A certain ringtone. Some practices.

Rituals? Like what I've been doing in the morning, saying stuff into spoon to make me a better learner and a better friend.

You've been doing that?

No diff than you looking into your mirror in your journal and writing things that matter to you. Plus, we've been doing the Questlisting checks a lot.

A talisman. That's what it's called. Something to remind a person of their commitment.

My grandfather's friend had a bracelet once. An ankle bracelet to track him.

Not funny, Stel.

My grandpa had an elastic band around his wrist. He would pull it every time he wanted a smoke. I can't remember when it disappeared.

I never smelled smoke at your grandpa's house.

Then the bracelet must have worked.

We need a non-conformist bracelet.

A being ourselves bracelet. Make it positive not negative.

Good one, Stella.

There's a rack of beaded bracelets for sale at the entrance to the campground where Pinky checks people in. Some of them have little bells on them.

Do you think that talking to ourselves in the morning when we look at ourselves, me in journal mirror and you in spoon, and wearing a bracelet will be enough to remind us to be true to our values? But what are our values?

It's a start. We know we have grown and are braver than ever. And that we are understanding the role of phones and social media, and self-worth. We can keep learning. Bonus for me, I'll wear it when I'm at the drug store. A bracelet would be a self-alarm if I feel the urge to lift something.

Hey, we're recording here. Where are you going? You just said something incredibly profound.

To get our remembering bracelets. I'll meet you at work.

ADDITIONAL NOTES IN JOURNAL

Everyone wants to be liked and to fit in. Pressure to fit in includes:

- Unspoken peer pressure: when you are exposed to actions of your peers and are left to choose whether you want to follow along… and don't always realize how strong the influence is.

- Negative peer pressure: when you are asked to engage in a behavior that is against your moral code or values (and you are threatened to be kicked out of the group if you don't do it).
- Positive peer pressure: when a friend or group of friends has a healthy influence on your life.
- I want to be with people who want to touch the stars.

12. STELLA SHARES A SECRET

Aurora, my name is on that egg salad sandwich if it does not sell in the next hour.

Pinky left a thermos of stew for us before she left for wherever she goes most evenings. I never had her marked as a bingo player.

She's not going to bingo. She gets back too early for that. Stew or no stew, I'm still having the egg salad. It's not just my brain that needs feeding, you know.

Maybe she's feeding the homeless. Or visiting a sick relative.

She goes for chemotherapy and some other treatments.

You knew this and you didn't tell me?

Are we going to have another argument?

And lookee here, we're at work in the concession so you can't run away from it.

Hey, I'm wearing my jingly bracelet. Third bell from the clasp—respond, do not react.

Some other Pinky wisdom?

No, I made it up myself. I was going to tell you.

Tell me about the bracelet, Pinky's cancer, or both?

Oh, Aurora, pul-ease. You didn't plug the phones in and kept it from me. Ring a bell?

You're right. I didn't tell you about the phones, but I was going to. But Stel, the Pinky thing is important.

I overheard. She didn't tell me. So, no matter how close I am to you, I made a decision to keep it to myself. Accidentally overhearing something should be kept private, even if it hurts, unless it's a life-or-death thing or someone is being abused. I should never say something that would affect the way you hang out with her. It's been painful to keep it to myself.

And you just changed your mind and told me now.

I wasn't holding it in confidence based on someone asking me to keep it private. This was mine to decide if and when to share, just like it is hers. I'd want you to do the same. People need to have fences around the stuff they know.

Stella, you blow my mind. Sometimes you are so smart. I can't write all this down. I'm going to dictate into the phone, and I'll write it all later. Maybe Sam and Magdalena have a computer I can type into.

It's recording. Let me refill our iced teas.

Sometimes conflict is best handled by dealing with it. Avoidance is the absolute most awful way to try to go through life.

I used to be the queen of avoidance.

Hey, I'm recording. But go on. Used to be?

Well, until a few days ago. Her majesty Stella. I sat high on my throne of avoidance, and it got me nowhere.

So, how did you change it? And, I add, it is recent, you could revert.

Listen. Did you hear that? It was your bracelet jingling. Bell number one. Stop being negative. We get what we think about.

Here's the egg salad sandwich, your award for "change your thoughts, change your life." Enjoy it, the eggs were from free-range hens.

I leaned.

You mean you learned. But how?

No, I leaned. I leaned into the uncomfortable.

Let me double check this is recording. I have a feeling you're about to state a brilliant brilliant. You know, when something amazing is fantastic.

Conflict is never comfortable, so lean into it. Breathe. Sit down with the other person you are having conflict with and talk it out, girl.

What about when the conflict is within?

Hey, you can sit and role play. Not like the other self is going to run away from you.

Talk. It. Out. Either inside yourself or with someone if they are willing to talk it out calmly.

A lot of conflict comes out of assuming. We guess what other peoples' motives could be. And we're usually wrong. We take action based on false beliefs.

I remember Miss Frankie saying there is an art to compromise and negotiation. Until you learn how to compromise, you will have a hard time resolving conflict. You can't win them all. Sometimes the only way to resolve conflict is to give the other person what they want. It's called choosing your battles. It may not feel fair to give in to the other person, but life isn't always fair. The sooner you understand that the quicker you will reach the pinnacle, like the peak, the very top, of thriving.

I don't really like that. I mean I get it, but does it mean then that you'd add some fences? Figure out how you got to that position in the first place, so you don't get there again. Maybe the person is someone you can let go of. Maybe not. I don't know if I like you can't win them all, Aurora. I don't like the competitive part. If I give the other person what they want, then aren't I going against my values?

If it's a bully, then it's not a conflict, if that's where you're going. That's different. That's when you're going to analyze your boundaries and who you're hanging with. But let's say it's you and me. We care about each other. Then let's say I really wanted that egg salad sandwich too. If I said that then, there could be a bit of a "well, you got the last one" fight. Or there could be a resolution in "let's share." Or I could just have not said anything at all, knowing that's not the hill I want to die on; that I want you to have the egg salad sandwich.

Oh no, Aurora, do you want the egg salad sandwich? There's no argument there.

You can have it all. Unless you want to share it.

It's not about the sandwich. But that's so nice of you to say. If I had wanted it and you wanted it, I would have said the same. We share. But I mean between people who are in conflict about bigger things. And egos. And attitudes. When it's all the egg salad sandwich it might be easy, but what about when it's the children in divorce, or a country in a war? What if it's about all the egg salad sandwiches?

Are you saying war is mayonnaise?

I'm saying food is power.

What does that even mean?

For now, it means even the most complex things people argue about can be melted down to something basic and simple.

Like mayonnaise?

Yes, Stella. Like mayonnaise.

Today's our last day. The campsite student program ends.

You get picked up by Sam and Magdalena. Then I take over the concession myself. Owl's organized a barbecue. He asked me for my grandpa's phone number. I feel badly the book is not done.

The book won't be done for a long time. A book isn't written in a week. It's not even written when it's finished because people who read it keep, well, writing it… in a way. I can keep up the work on it in the summer while I'm at the farm, reincarnating Tree. We'll find time for me to call you here, when you're at the concession, but not when you're helping Owl with Pinky, now that she's asked for some help.

Notice nothing is talking to us since we started writing that book?

Oh, I think it is, Stel. Just in a different way.

So, I was thinking this… if changing your thoughts changes your life, does living your life change the world?

Give me a minute.

It has to be true.

Let's say you live from a negative point of view. Do you change the world?

I think we have to change the statement, Stel. Changing to positive thoughts will change your life to a more positive life. Living your life positively, from a place of love, kindness, and respect, changes the world into a more wondrous place.

That's why you're the writer.

That's really nice, Stel. But we're all writers. You inspired that statement. Someone else might improve it. One family. One collective.

Aurora, can you keep a secret, now? Why do I ask? I know you can. Can I tell you something? I've been talking to spoon. You knew that. I've been recording it. It doesn't even sound like me. Don't freak out. I mean I know it's me, but it's like through me. I figure if I record enough, and listen to them, I'll grow even more. And we could record for each other, while we're apart for the rest of the summer. I'll keep my job here and ask if I can stay in Pinky and Owl's spare room, then split my time between here and Grandpa's. I know I should have told you but I was working it all out. In my head. Me. I know. I've surprised myself. I want to be a speaker.

You are smart. Wow. And a speaker is perfect. You have the most amazing, lovable voice because you keep it real. You meet people where they're at. Do they have jobs for speakers?

Remember Zonda the incredible makeup girl on YouTube? I could have my own channel. But I'd talk about deeper things than cosmetics. Not that there's anything wrong with cosmetics. I'd talk about respecting all people's journeys. I'd invite guests. Ask questions. Maybe I'd be on the news too. Investigative reporter. But for the next while, I could work on having a channel and still do the concession and help Owl and Pinky, and be there for Grandpa, and go to school. And I'll still hold the stars every night.

You won't have time for the phone.

The girl with the spoon. I'll get everyone to carry spoons and see themselves upside down. I'll get everyone Questlisting and questioning.

And turn their lives upside down you mean.

And you'll be my first guest and talk about journals.

Are you going to let me listen to what came through you?

Here, hit play. And by the way, you can do this too, Aurora. Got some feelings in the night? Hit record. Hear someone say something you want to remember? Yep. One tap.

You've got a lot of recordings.

I've been busy.

THE RECORDING BY STELLA

Testing, testing. One, two, three. Looks like it's working. Okay. Who is in charge of your emotions? I will answer that for you. You are. You are in charge of your feelings. While we cannot control what happens in our lives, we can master, that means ace, how we experience or react to these events.

I am only a teenager but, for a long time now, I have

blamed other people for my poor choices. I know I am lucky to have escaped some dangerous situations, and I credit my friend Aurora for that… and my grandpa. These last ten days, most of it without a phone, much of it in the outdoors, and every night under the stars, I realized that I am responsible for my choices and for the way I handle "stuff." I know I used to react. React like a whole bucket of firecrackers. I've found peace in responding instead. There is a difference—there are no matches or explosions.

My saying it was someone else's fault brought me to the edge of being a victim. He did this. She left me. They don't like teenagers. Poor me.

All of that made it impossible to be positive, to see goodness, to feel goodness. Yes, some things happen outside my control. No matter how positive I am, stuff will go down and not be pleasant as in a poop show. The old me would have sworn here, but there has appeared an elegance to my thoughts that flow through to my speaking voice. I want my voice to be like the night sky and my words to reflect the stars. I have no problem if others swear, curse, rant, rave, but I have set a new standard for myself. It will make me different. But I do it not for attention of others. I do it to bring the most positive words to myself. It's something I feel is important.

Why did you hit stop, Aurora? It's not over. You're just getting to the good bits.

I have to tell you. I read about this study by a Japanese scientist, Dr. Emoto. He photographed water—like super close-up under a microscope. Some of the water had been yelled at and hated with words and feelings. Some other water had been sent positive vibes with soft talk and words of love. The differences between the images under the microscope were huge. The pattern of the unloved water was chaotic and spattered. The pattern on the loved water was like a mandala or flower. Maybe it's the same for your word choices. Just sayin', Stella. You might be doing that experiment with words instead of water. Sorry I interrupted.

Which is cool. And you'll see why. And I will look it up. Push play and keep listening.

Nova

BACK TO THE RECORDING OF STELLA

It's as if, when the positive words, the gentle thoughts, the kindness is in me, I am a softer place for myself to fall into. I am like a smooth painting inside with a design that pleases me. I feel jagged and disconnected when the words are negative, and, for me, when I swear. Yet I was such a potty mouth two weeks ago.

The question is, when you get knocked down, are you going to allow that to shape your life or are you going to use it to empower you through life? Your response will determine the outcome, not just for you but for others.

To the people who might be listening to this, if it was a podcast or on a YouTube channel:

Self-talk has a massive impact on our emotions and feelings. We seem to be made—as in biologically wired—to prepare ourselves for the worst-case scenario. We forget that we are the authors of our own stories.

The choice is ours. What sort of self-talk are you going to allow? You get to choose happiness in some form in every situation. Even in grief. Even at the graveyard when you stand over the stone of your mother and cry that things could have been different. You can release yourself to some form of positive. Catch a glance at the robin sitting on a branch watching you. Wipe your runny nose on a Kleenex and imagine the hand is that of all the loving people in the world caring about you.

Don't wait to be old, like thirty, before you start making decisions to go forward in life. Do it now, even if you are thirteen. Do it if you are sixteen. And if you are, like, twenty-five, that's okay, just do it. Or if you happened upon this advice by mistake and you're older than thirty, well, I don't know what that's like, but I pretty much feel you can change your thoughts and change your life at any time you are breathing. You can even do something that leaves a legacy so that you are doing something after you stop breathing.

The only one holding you back from achieving everything you want in life is you. You are in charge of your life, and you are in charge of your feelings. The only one responsible for working hard for the things you want, and finding balance, so you don't work so hard that you burn out, is you. The only one responsible for how you respond to difficult times is you. You are responsible for you. Whatever controls your mind, controls your choices.

Now this is pretty big of me to say because I should be saying it only for myself. But I would like you to say it to yourself, and use "I" where it says you. And try those thoughts on for size. Record them in your phone with your voice and your name or "I," and at least sample what that feels like.

You can shut it off now, Aurora. Did it sound stupid? Am I crazy for wanting to speak to the world? Even if it's only myself that listens?

Especially if it is your own self that listens... first. You're going to have a massive following. More than Zonda, queen of makeup.

I'm not competing. I'm happy to have her on my show.

Listen to you. My show. I love it.

13. THE COURAGE TO RISE

Aurora, when you get data on your phone, or when you're at Sam and Magdalena's and using their internet, check out University of California, Berkeley.

Berkeley? You're ambitious huh?

No, hear me out. It's about something online.

There was this link to Berkeley. There's an online course. FREE. For people like us, you know, teenagers, it's called the "Science and Practice of Happiness." I thought it would be good if we took it together while you're at the farm and woodworking and I'm here.

Aurora, turn on the recorder. You have more juice in yours than I have in mine.

It seems an insult to the stars to record under them.

Who the heck do you think has been feeding us all this information, Aurora? The stars are where all this is coming from, or some superpower beyond the stars, some superpower who made the stars. God.

From the stars?

From the collective. From a higher power. From within ourselves and from without ourselves. From God.

Stella, you are like a philosopher.

Now I know why I said Aristotle before. Grandpa told me if I had been a boy, Grandpa they were going to name me that.

It's recording. Now what?

I don't know, you're the brainiac.

Nova

But you said to turn on the recording app.

Because that's what my intuition told me. I had no idea what I was going to say. Or you. So go... I don't think we have to whisper anymore. Everyone within ten miles is fast asleep.

Who would have known our quest, our sleep-out in the campground on student week, where hardly any students even showed up, and we had the campsite almost to ourselves, would have turned out to be such a... such a...

Profound experience?

Such a profound experience. The stars, Tree, the stories, standing up for what we thought was right, the meeting other people, jobs, plans, IHOP, the no-phone lessons.

Profound.

Stella and the spoon.

Don't forget the strawberry place. Bernie is unfinished business for you.

Closer to our purpose? You are, Stel. You have a vision of sharing a message. You're all set for a broadcasting career, and you've got a podcast or YouTube channel in the wings.

On the wings.

Of angels?

All voices are spiritual, Aurora.

You went to church yesterday with Pinky, didn't you?

It was on the way to Costco. We worshipped at both altars—the big-box retail altar and the churchy one.

What was it like?

They had samples of salami. And some of those fishy crackers.

Nova

You know I meant the church.

A lot of fellowship and community. Not what I expected, but you have to stay tuned for that.

Pinky found peace in the church? What about Owl?

They each have their own faith. Pinky says God is love. Owl says Nature is Lord. After they said that to me, they smiled at each other.

Do God and Nature smile at each other too?

You found your inner activist.

Tree hugger for a day. But I think it's sticking. Enough of me. Stella, if this was a podcast, what would you say to others on how to find their purpose?

You have to help me with that.

Let's take turns.

It's still recording?

Ninety-eight percent charged.

How many stars are up there?

That's not advice, it's a question.

That might be the title of my podcast.

I think you need a subheading

How about "the courage to rise"?

It has potential. But you're such an interesting, erm, person, I would vote for Stella the Spoon. It has a ring to it. Now, stop stalling, Stella. Do the first. Dig deep in that amazingly quirky brain of yours and answer this: How do people find their purpose?

We're always finding purpose. Don't even try to understand that, but...

Nova

One. Be still and listen.

Our lives are full of noise. Social media, Netflix, school, work. When not in balance, these things clutter our minds. We allow them to clutter our minds. It's not their fault. It's our choice to bring ourselves unlimited joy. Hint... social media 24/7 is not unlimited joy. Make sure to tune in to my channel. Prioritize me. No, seriously, choose what speaks to you and prioritize wisely.

Your turn. Blow my mind. And then let's do a title for your book... which, by the way, I think you already did.

Two. Once you are still, then open your mind. Explore within and decide what excites you. Combine that with what your gut says—what the world needs more of. Do what you love to do when you are the most authentically happy.

Over to you, Stella.

Three. Connect with yourself. And don't make the mirror an enemy.

All the answers are inside you. It's inside ourselves that we make ourselves stronger. When we take time to reflect and listen within, we get to know ourselves better. You will get closer to finding your purpose. What is Stella the Spoon talking about, you ask?

Look for clues. Try things. Feel the fear and do or say it anyway if it is not hurtful to others. Listen first, then speak up, speak out, sing the song of the sun if you want to. Be unapologetically you.

When you have confidence, positive self-talk, a healthy body image, are kind to others and yourself, and have gratitude for everything—even some of the yucky stuff that turns out to be lessons, then you are totally okay. And then you can be even more open to understanding faith.

PINKY ARRIVES

Girls, sorry to interrupt. I couldn't sleep. And I did overhear a bit of your conversation. You should be sharing this with others your age. Or all ages.

Tomorrow everything changes. I wanted to say something to you both on this last night:

You are both diamonds.

Diamonds are created under extreme heat and pressure from the earth. Diamonds are the hardest mineral we know of. This precious and valuable mineral didn't just happen, it was formed, over time.

Replace the earth's extreme heat and pressure by emotional extreme "heat" and "pressure." Advertising hooks: buy-now-pay-later, this-will-make-you-younger, this-will-make-you-real. Add to that peer pressure, difficult situations, and challenges of every kind you can imagine.

All these make you real: patience, tolerance, moving forward, not being afraid to mess up, letting people flow in and out of your life with grace—that means being nice to them all; you can still be nice to people you don't like. Being kind is a service to the world. It helps cultivate goodness so that others can grow at whatever rate is possible for them. Mostly, and more importantly, from this kindness, you will grow.

Imagine the stars twinkling in the sky, then you and many others on the earth as diamonds, reflecting each other. Deep, peaceful, powerful, bright.

Imagine your strength builds confidence and then your confidence building more strength, all from rebounding from things that seemingly didn't work out, as well as things that do. Change up your actions until you find solutions that are born from peace. Confidence comes from success. Success comes from lots of fails that aren't fails but growths… restarts, begin-agains.

When you are the diamond, no matter what tries to break you, it cannot.

You become unstoppable. No matter the form you are in. Tree knew that. I know that too.

With very step forward: wiser, kinder, more magical.

Goodnight girls.

Nova

Aurora, is it still recording? We should have told her.

That diamond part must be super powerful. The phone's down to seventy-five percent. That's still plenty for more thoughts though. It's our last night.

There's something you told me before we started on this thing. I think you said it was a something quest.

A Vision Quest, Stel.

The laser tag place at Washington and Seventh?

Vison Quest. The power of mental imaging.

I know, I was just joking. Humor is important. Our conversations are getting heavy, and tomorrow is our last day.

It's already tomorrow.

See, Aurora, a charged phone is useful for telling the time as well.

You'll have data before the end of next week. But I know you'll use the power wisely.

Tell me about vision. Be my guest. The floor, as in the earth under our sleeping bags, is yours, Aurora.

I want to write about it in the book.

We can be a team. YouTube or podcast, and the book. A workbook even.

Look at us, this is the visualization I was talking about.

Meaning?

We are imagining. Wait, let me show you. Your eyes are closed right?

What color is the electronic banner under the graphic on your YouTube channel?

Green. Like life. Like a tree's leaves in spring. Fresh green. Bright, fresh green. Not neon. Not snot. Not puke.

You can see it?

Fresh, green, leaf-green.

Okay, keep that in the lens. Where will you YouTube from?

Pinky's spare room has a freshly painted beige wall. Very neutral.

Can you see yourself in front of it? Of course you can. You just described the wall. Now, Stel, what is in front of you?

A laptop. I can't tell if it's a Mac. An external mic and camera. A glass of water, so my voice stays fresh. Paper and a pen. I can see it all now. It's all on a wooden desk that has two drawers on the right side.

Where did you buy the laptop?

I paid for it week-by-week at Better Compute on Fourth Street, but... but... When the guy there knew what I was going to do, he discounted it to cost and traded the other equipment for mention of his store.

Stel, you've painted it so well, I'm there. He's that guy with the facial hair but you can still see that big smile, right?

That's him. He's the manager there but he used to be the assistant. He says I can work there when the concession closes in the winter. And, wait, what's that? He says only for one season because he thinks I'll be making an income from YouTubing by then.

Stella: I give you visualization.

It's going to work. You created the scene in your mind of what you want to happen. Now, you'll work toward it, rolling with small changes, tweaking the plan as you go. As you go with it, your energy will be so high, that others will feel it and help you. Then, you can help others.

I'm going to get some pictures and put them together in a collage and keep adding. I'm going to include a college diploma, a blue car, and please don't think this is morbid, but a proper headstone for my mother's grave. And a massive cold-cuts basket for my grandpa.

Stella, the only thing morbid there is the gift basket; that's a lot of pig and cow.

I do believe my sense of humor is rubbing off on you.

I wasn't joking. That much processed meat can't be good for an old man.

You crack me up. Now what are you going to laser quest?

It's late. I'm tired.

Don't flake out on me. We're on air.

Okay, okay, I've got a massive list typing on white

paper in my head, I need to pause that and turn to the image beside it. I'll read the list after. This is what I see: I'm standing at the top of a mountain. My hair is alive at its reddest and longest. My right hand holds a spear. A heart shield in the other. I am the age I am now, in this moment, but I look like I'm from another century. There is a daisy chain circle on my head. A bridled white horse stands behind me. Its head is dropped to fresh green grass the same color as your logo. Behind its saddle are blankets and food for those who are in need. My feet are bare, and soft bluebells poke through my toes. They smell like cut grass, and because I don't know what bluebells smell like, they are in my nose as lilacs.

And typed by the keys of an old black typewriter:

She chooses not to waste her energy on foolishness.

She is a guardian, a nurturer; wise beyond her years.

She has a heart as big as oceans and will always face her fears.

Nova

She rises from the ashes.

She doesn't seek revenge; she moves on and lets karma do the work.

She is sculpted by her pain and struggles to become her own hero.

Stella, it's so close I can touch it: confidence, positive self-talk and body image, kindness, gratitude, and a belief system.

Aurora, I have no words. I need time to take it all in... In your vision, do you see yourself returning to the old strawberry farm?

It isn't old anymore. I find the owner. A grumpy old guy who just needs company. I somehow arrange for new plants to be set.

Rocking chair on a broken porch, right?

I introduce him to your grandpa.

Oh, that sounds like fun.

I see it clearly.

And Bernice, is she there?

I meet her in a safe space. With Magdalena. Maybe even my social worker after I tell her I think Bernice and I may be related, apologize for my AWOL status, and reassure her I am not a runner anymore.

What's it look like?

I am sitting on an uncomfortable chair and do lots of breaths in and out, and then ask Bernice what happened to her sister. I ask her to tell me again about the last time they saw each other, and her sister was going to have a baby. And then I sit very still and bite my lips together and hold your hand under the table and wait for her to respond.

Aurora, are you sleeping?

No, I've been listing to you mumble, or I thought you were talking while I was working. I thought I was dreaming. Why do you have to do things in the middle of the night?

Okay I want you to try something. Wake up. You'll still have a few hours after this. Just listen to what I've recorded on my phone and on yours because I was running out of power.

Testing, testing, One, two, three. It's working. Hello listener. If you're reading this on a post, then press record on your phone and read it aloud slowly. If you're listening to it on your phone, then play this often.

Copyright, Stella the Spoon.

AFFIRMATION – GUIDED MEDITATION – THE WARRIOR

Look into your spoon or little mirror or up at the stars as you repeat the first part, then close your eyes when directed.

I am created for change.

I can be the change I want to see in the world.

I am a trailblazer.

Close your eyes.

Imagine walking along a path. A long one that takes an entire day to travel. One you know will lead you to everything you have envisioned for your life, and more. Look down. What is the path made of? Is it paved or dirt or stone? What about your feet? Are you wearing shoes or runners or sandals? Are you barefoot?

What is beside the path? Fence, wall, building, grasses, shrubs, trees, or all of these things? What can you smell in the air?

Stick out your tongue; what can you taste?

Someone was the first person to make this path. How long ago you do not know, but there is history—someone walked before you—many walked before you—along this route.

Stretch out your arms. Feel the air against your hands.

Suddenly the path ends and there is only a dense forest. Not one piece of groundcover has a footprint. Not one leaf has been disturbed.

You have three choices. Go back. Go forward. Stay where you are.

If you turn back, you will not experience the life you wanted. You will, after a long journey back, have what you had and be where you were.

Nova

If you stay in one place, you will get tired of waiting for something to change. You will be the stagnant pond, slowly drying. No flow, no fresh, no source.

Or you can take one step into the woods, the first of many that will create your own trail. There will be streams to cross, maybe rivers, there might be wild animals, there will be times when you have to make your own shelter to stay out of the rain, and there will be a constant building of strength as you create your own route and leave it open for others to follow.

Take the step. Open your mouth wide, stick out your tongue, and roar like the lioness you are.

You are no longer following a path, you are creating one.

You are a trailblazer.

You are a leader.

You are not alone. When you get to your destination, you will meet others who have carved out paths in those same woods and other woods. And you will know there will be people who come to the end of that first path and follow yours. You are an influencer. You are a pioneer. You are grateful for the first path to follow, and equally grateful to have the opportunity to collaborate, cooperate, and create.

You are the trailblazer.

You are the warrior.

You are the change.

Be silent for a bit. Keep your eyes closed. What do you look like in your vision? What will you call yourself?

Open your eyes.

Look into your mirror and repeat:

I am a trailblazer.

I am called: _____.

Testing, testing. I know this works.

Hi, I'm Stella from Stella and the Spoon.

Remember, if you're reading this on somebody's feed, then read it aloud, nice and slowly into your device. Keep it handy to listen to.

I am curious. An explorer of life and love.

I am a researcher

Of happiness.

I am an explorer.

Of possibilities.

This is only possible by asking questions.

And listening to the answers.

Weighing them all on the scale in my heart.

Questions grow me.

I love being curious.

I love being a researcher.

I love being an explorer.

Nova

Hello, Stella of Stella the Spoon here. You know what to do.

Courtesy of the lessons I learned from Aurora, and her mentor, Miss Frankie. every person is worthy of any prize on the shelf.

Look into your spoon or little mirror. Repeat:

I am strong and confident because I listen to my gut.

I march to the beat of my own heart.

I am open to the rhythm of others.

I am interesting (to others) and interested (in others).

I have the confidence to sit at any table.

And the strength to walk away.

My superpower is love, and through self-love I can respond to any situation.

If I were at a fairground, tossing rings around the necks of bottles, my hands would not shake. I would have a big smile on my face. And the white teddy bear, too large to fit properly on the top shelf, would be smiling back. And at that moment, I know I already have every prize on the shelf. Whether that bear comes home with me or I give him to someone else or my rings land between the bottles and teddy remains in the tent. I am about contributing, playing, laughter, and cheering others on.

I am strong and confident because I listen to my gut.

I march to the beat of my own heart.
I am open to the rhythm of others.
I am interesting (to others) and interested (in others).
I have the confidence to sit at any table.
And the strength to walk away.

My superpower is love, and through self-love I can respond to any situation.

Wow, Stella. Just wow.

Wow yourself, Aurora.

Stella the Spoon.

I like it. It's quirky. Like me. Now what about you?

What about me?

Look at us. Sunrise, sunset, the stars. Our names. Aurora like the northern lights, and Stella like planetary and space. Remember Ms. Milner in science, grade five?

Nova

What happened to you learned nothing in school?

There's this kind of star that suddenly releases a huge burst of energy, so it becomes this fantasmagorical light. It's called a nova.

Nova also means new. Mrs. Patterson. Grade seven. English.

Aurora, your book. Nova: The Courage to Rise.

14. AURORA AND STELLA MAKE A PACT

Your grandpa and Owl are sure hitting it off, huh?

I've never seen him put his arm around another guy's shoulders since his friend with the ankle bracelet croaked.

I'll email you tonight from the farm's computer.

I'll text you tomorrow when I'm back on my phone plan.

Everyone's giving us space. They're such good people.

Room to say goodbye.

Stella, this is not goodbye. This is hello world. Hello self. Hello future. Hello change. I am going to make peace with my past and move on to my purpose. You're going to get that YouTube going. I need you to be my accountability partner.

Aurora, I don't do math. I'm not an accountant.

Stop joking. You know what I mean. We share, we encourage, we support, we even report to each other where we're at in our plans. We brainstorm. We suggest.

Answerability partners. Inspirational partners.

Were you as surprised as me to learn Pastor Jamieson is Maggie's mother?

This world is getting smaller by the minute.

Look at us. We've changed.

Confidence. Check. Positive self-talk. Mostly check.

Positive body image. Check. Got my hair all braided and told my freckles I loved them just like I love Anne Shirley's. Kindness. Check. See it in so many and keep giving it back.

Gratitude. Check. I'm just thanking the world, the universe, even God, for this quest.

Faith. Check. I'm on the train. Following the pastor's route. And that feels good.

Check. Us. Out. Questlisting.

Stel, I don't want this hug to end. Yet I'm excited to let go as well. Know what I mean?

Go. The carpenter is already in his truck. Magdalena is holding Freedom on her hip, and I've got a concession to open, an employee to train, then I'm headed to chemo with Pinky.

Hold your vision, Stella. Text me every night and ask me how many stars there are up there because, when you ask, you're holding me.

LETTER TO THE READER 2

Like Stella, my grandfather played a huge role in my upbringing. My grandmother too.

When I was eight years old, my grandfather loaded up his van with sacks of groceries and invited me to come along for the ride.

We stopped in front of the tiniest house I had ever seen. As we made our way to the front door, sobbing and crying filled the air. My grandfather knocked. I stood, frozen, unable to conjure up an explanation for the misery I could feel oozing through the cracks under the door and through the thin walls.

A small girl, perhaps three years old, opened the door. Her little face was streaked with fresh tears. When she saw our arms filled with sacks of groceries, she stopped crying, wiped her eyes, and said, "Food?"

Inside we found four children, the oldest a girl who appeared to be about nine. There were no parents present.

The wailing stopped as each child in turn saw the goods we'd brought—canned beans, powdered milk, cereal, dried soups, pasta, rice, pasta sauce, and canned tomatoes.

I had never witnessed hunger or poverty like this before. It changed me forever.

In the basement of my grandparents' home was a bedroom-sized room that we called the pantry. The walls were lined with shelves which were filled with food. They did this for one reason: when someone knocked on their door and asked for help, my grandparents had a stock of food to give. They were, in those years, the equivalent of a successful outreach program. A non-denominational, not-for-profit, humble organization of two people who loved others unconditionally.

My grandparents are the reason I pursued my passion for serving those who need someone to listen, a shoulder to lean on, a friend to support an idea, funds to restart, a wall to bounce a thousand balls of ideas off.

I've had the honor of getting to know girls just like Aurora. Girls who may not have had the connection they wanted from a mother, or parents, for a variety of reasons. Some of these girls have come through the foster system, some living with other family members, and some simply in a home with parents too busy working several jobs just to put food on the table or dealing with issues that eclipse their ability to parent effectively.

When I came up with the idea for this book, it was to find a way to help girls like Stella and Aurora—and you—learn to see the potential in themselves and their futures. To learn that you already have what you need, whatever your circumstances or your past. I hope you may find the inspiration in Stella and Aurora's Questlisting to embark on your own quest and that you discover, in the process, that there is indeed beauty in everything, we just have to make a choice to see it.

And speaking of beauty in everything, that's the name of my foundation: The Beauty in Everything Foundation. Here, we are committed to the development of girls and young women by giving them access to resources and the tools girls need to *thrive*.

We are obsessed with showing girls they are amazing, they are warriors, and to help them dream big dreams. Then we give them the tools to achieve those dreams. We are a group of passionate, driven, hard-working, and generous women who won't stop until we inspire and empower a group of girls (a large group of girls, an insanely large group of girls) to be passionate, driven, hard-working, kind, and courageous. That is our goal. Our goal is to inspire and empower girls to think they breathe fire. Fire like Aurora's streaming, flaming, gorgeous hair and Stella's new-found burning desire to share with others what she discovered by speaking into her reflection in the spoon and turning that into a podcast.

Ready for your own quest? Go forth and breathe fire.

Love, Tricia

ACKNOWLEDGMENTS

I'm thankful to my family and friends for your endless enthusiasm for this project, but especially my mom, Audrey, whose encouragement lifted me out of many writing blocks.

I am also grateful to Marie Beswick Arthur, who took my vision of weaving in the life lessons I so passionately want my readers to be inspired by and made this story sing. You brought a level of creativity and storytelling to the characters' narrative that was beyond my imagination. This wouldn't be what it is without you.

A massive thanks to my publisher, Boni Wagner-Stafford at Ingenium Books, who believed in me in a big way and helped me navigate this process with patience and ease. Your meticulous attention to detail and thoughtful edits polished the manuscript beautifully and brought this project to fruition.

And so, God said, "Let Tricia have two angels as escorts," and He sent Boni and Marie.

I'm eternally grateful to my husband and daughters who inspired me in the most profound ways and gave me the space to complete this project when it felt impossible. Every day is made sweeter by your presence.

To Greg, whose quiet strength gives wind to my sails.

To my daughters Kailey, Reagan, Grace, and Allie. Being your mom is the greatest honor of my life.

And to Christ, my Savior, the ultimate source of strength and the root of anything that goes well.

ABOUT THE AUTHOR

Tricia is a social entrepreneur, writer, blogger, finance veteran, and fierce child advocate. Founder of the children's clothing brand, Crossing Arrows and Beauty in Everything Foundation, she has been involved throughout her community through charitable organizations with most of her volunteer work focused on child advocacy.

Throughout the growth of Crossing Arrows, Tricia realized she wanted to inspire and empower girls on a larger platform and so the Beauty in Everything Foundation was created. She plans to use her leadership background and passion to empower girls to be courageous, kind, and to thrive in this journey we call life.

Made in the USA
Coppell, TX
15 November 2021